Mezzo-Soprano/Alto/Belter

MW01493210

THE
SINGER'S
MUSICAL THEATRE
ANTHOLOGY

A collection of songs from musicals, categorized by voice type, in authentic settings, specifically selected for teens.

Compiled and Edited by Richard Walters

ISBN: 978-1-4234-7672-6

HAL•LEONARD®
CORPORATION

7777 W. BLUEMOUND RD. P.O. BOX 13819 MILWAUKEE, WI 53213

Visit Hal Leonard Online at
www.halleonard.com

Foreword

Over the years several teachers have made requests to me for something just for teens in *The Singer's Musical Theatre Anthology* series. This volume attempts to address the needs of those teachers and their students. Another equally important factor in the genesis of this Teen's Edition has been the repeated experience of hearing young performers attempt to sing material that is unsuitable to them, both vocally and dramatically. There are no firm rules about what musical theatre literature is appropriate for teen singers, and individual talents certainly vary. Nevertheless, some reasonable guidelines were applied in the selection of material for the Teen's Edition, cited below.

The music should be vocally appropriate for a young voice.

To draw a parallel, in the study of classical voice young singers do not begin with dramatic arias by Wagner and Verdi. The same is true for theatre music. Most teenage women would quickly get into serious vocal trouble if they attempt to regularly sing with what could be described as a "big chest belt." While an easy, buoyant, lyrical belt is natural for many voices, and part of theatre style, songs that encourage more dramatic and extreme range belting, which can harm a still maturing vocal apparatus, have been avoided in this volume.

The song and the role should be dramatically appropriate for a young performer.

"Appropriate for a young performer" does not mean that all the songs in this book are sung by teenage characters in the original show contexts, but if not the characters are young adults. Some teens certainly attempt to play older character or dramatic roles at times, but generally, most young performers are most flattered by and most comfortable with songs written for young characters.

The collection includes a variety of songs and styles, from classic to contemporary.

There is a common phenomenon of the young musical theatre enthusiast only interested in recent shows. Musical theatre has a vast, valuable heritage that needs to be explored. Additionally, young performers will only fully discover versatility as a singing actor by broadening their repertory to include classic songs from shows written in the middle decades of the 20th century.

Songs are presented in authentic editions.

Standard piano/vocal (or piano/vocal/guitar) sheet music has long been the general format for popular and theatre music. This format is very important for a song to find the widest possible uses, especially with millions of amateur pianists. But these simplified sheet music editions of show music, often transposed and with the melody in the piano part, are not the best source for a singing actor. *The Singer's Musical Theatre Anthology* series has always attempted to present the music as it was originally performed, with authentic accompaniment.

Songs are presented in the original keys.

Almost all songs in this Mezzo-Soprano/Alto/Belter collection are presented in original keys, with these exceptions:

"In My Own Little Corner" has been sung in different keys in three television productions. To make it vocally accessible to many singers it appears here a whole-step lower than published in the *Cinderella* vocal score. "What I've Been Looking For" has been shifted into a comfortable key, and adapted from its original duet form into a solo version. The original Broadway key for "My New Philosophy" was unusually high, to accommodate the unique voice of Kristen Chenoweth. As a belted song the original key is simply out of reach for 99% of performers; we transposed it down for vocal access.

I appreciate and acknowledge Joel Boyd's participation in developing the Teen's Edition. I especially thank assistant editor Joshua Parman for his work on this four-volume series, and also his diligent help in the recording studio in creating the companion audio accompaniments.

Richard Walters
Editor

THE SINGER'S MUSICAL THEATRE ANTHOLOGY

Mezzo-Soprano/Alto/Belter Teen's Edition

Contents

ABOUT THE SHOWS

ANNIE GET YOUR GUN

MUSIC AND LYRICS: Irving Berlin
BOOK: Herbert and Dorothy Fields
DIRECTOR: Joshua Logan
CHOREOGRAPHER: Helen Tamiris
OPENED: May 16, 1946, New York; a run of 1,147 performances

Irving Berlin's musical biography of scrappy gal sharpshooter Annie Oakley earned standing ovations for Broadway stars of two generations: the original, Ethel Merman, in the 1940s; Bernadette Peters and Reba McEntire in the 1990s. The tune-packed musical traces Annie's rise from illiterate hillbilly to international marksmanship star as she is discovered and developed in the traveling "Buffalo Bill's Wild West Show." She falls hard for the show's chauvinistic male star, Frank Butler. And romance blossoms until Annie begins to outshine Frank. Annie gets the chance to express her folksy philosophies in song. She proclaims the glories of the simple life in **"I Got the Sun in the Morning."**

BEAUTY AND THE BEAST

MUSIC: Alan Menken
LYRICS: Howard Ashman and Tim Rice
BOOK: Linda Woolverton
FILM DIRECTORS: Gary Trousdale and Kirk Wise
FILM SCREENPLAY: Linda Woolverton and Roger Allers
FILM RELEASED: November 22, 1991, Walt Disney Pictures
BROADWAY DIRECTOR: Robert Jess Roth
BROADWAY CHOREOGRAPHER: Matt West
BROADWAY OPENING: April 18, 1994, New York; a run of 5,461 performances

Disney made its Broadway debut with a big-budget adaptation of its own 1991 Oscar-nominated musical film. Like the classic fairy tale on which it is based, *Beauty and the Beast* tells the story of a witch who transforms a haughty prince into a fearsome Beast (and his servants into household objects). The spell can be broken only when the prince learns how to love, and how to inspire love. Lyricist Ashman died in 1991 before the film was released. The stage score includes several songs written for the film but not used, plus five new songs with lyrics by Broadway veteran Tim Rice. Headstrong young woman Belle discovers the Beast's castle after her father is captured and held prisoner there. She bravely offers to exchange herself for her father and soon finds herself adopted by the various living clocks, teapots, candlesticks, and cutlery who strive to match make their beastly boss and the eligible but understandably resistant maiden. In **"A Change in Me,"** Belle realizes that her feelings for the increasingly gentlemanly Beast are beginning to soften. The song was added to the show mid-run when pop diva Toni Braxton played Belle.

CATS

MUSIC: Andrew Lloyd Webber
LYRICS: T.S. Eliot
DIRECTOR: Trevor Nunn
CHOREOGRAPHER: Gillian Lynne
OPENED: May 11, 1981, London; a run of 8,949 performances
        October 7, 1982, New York; a run of 7,485 performances

Charged with energy, flair, and imagination, this feline fantasy proved to be equally successful on Broadway where it was even more of an environmental experience than in London's West End. With the entire Winter Garden theatre transformed into one enormous junkyard, theatergoers were confronted with such unexpected sights as outsized garbagy objects spilling into the audience, the elimination of the proscenium arch, and a lowered ceiling transformed into a twinkling canopy suggesting both cats' eyes and stars. Adapted from T.S. Eliot's collection of poems, *Old Possum's Book of Practical Cats*, the song-and-dance spectacle introduces such whimsical characters as the mysterious Mr. Mistoffelees, the patriarchal Old Deuteronomy, Skimbleshanks the Railway Cat, and Jennyanydots, the Old Gumbie Cat who sits all day and becomes active only at night. The musical's hit song, **"Memory,"** is sung by Grizabella, the faded Glamour Cat, who, at the evening's end, ascends to the cats' heaven known as the Heaviside Layer.

A CHORUS LINE

MUSIC: Marvin Hamlisch
LYRICS: Edward Kleban
BOOK: James Kirkwood and Nicholas Dante
DIRECTOR AND CHOREOGRAPHER: Michael Bennett
OPENED: April 15, 1975, New York; a run of 6,137 performances

Beginning with the deceptively simple premise of an audition for chorus dancers, *A Chorus Line* eventually proves to be an interesting examination of the dancer's thoughts and feelings, shown in monologues, dialogues, solo songs, and ensembles. Created as a workshop production in Joseph Papp's Public Theatre, the show, like *Company* and *Follies* before it, has no traditional plot, and has been widely imitated. *A Chorus Line* is one of the longest running productions in Broadway history. During the audition, one of the dancers is injured. Diana reflects that even if she could no longer dance, she has no regrets (**"What I Did for Love"**).

CINDERELLA
(television)

MUSIC: Richard Rodgers
LYRICS AND BOOK: Oscar Hammerstein II
DIRECTOR: Ralph Nelson
CHOREOGRAPHER: Jonathan Lucas
AIRED: March 31, 1957, CBS

Ever the innovators, Rodgers & Hammerstein were among the first to explore the new medium of television with a full-length original TV musical. The initial broadcast in 1957 starring Julie Andrews, drew the largest television audience to date of 107 million people. A new color television version was made in 1965, starring Lesley Ann Warren. The 1997 television film starred Brandy Norwood, with other songs by Rodgers interpolated into the score. Based on the fairy tale *Cinderella*, the musical follows the traditional story of a young woman who collaborates with her fairy godmother to overcome the plots of her evil stepmother and stepsisters so she can go to an opulent ball and meet a handsome prince. Abused and underappreciated by her stepmother and stepsisters, Cinderella sits by the fireplace alone and sings **"In My Own Little Corner."** The fairy godmother magically appears and enables Cinderella to attend the royal ball. At the ball, Cinderella's stepsisters do not recognize her after her fairytale makeover. They jealously sing **"Stepsisters' Lament"** as they eye the Prince's attention to the mysterious belle of the ball.

FINIAN'S RAINBOW

MUSIC: Burton Lane
LYRICS: E.Y. "Yip" Harburg
BOOK: E.Y. Harburg and Fred Saidy
DIRECTOR: Bretaigne Windust
CHOREOGRAPHER: Michael Kidd
OPENED: January 10, 1947, New York; a run of 725 performances

Finian's Rainbow evolved out of co-librettist E.Y. Harburg's desire to satirize an economic system that requires gold reserves to be buried in the ground at Fort Knox. This led to the idea of leprechauns and the crock of gold that, according to legend, could grant three wishes. The story takes place in Rainbow Valley, Missitucky, and involves Finian McLonergan, an Irish immigrant, and his efforts to bury a crock of gold which, he is sure, will grow and make him rich. Also involved are Og, a leprechaun from whom the crock has been stolen and Finian's daughter, Sharon, who wonders wistfully **"How Are Things in Glocca Morra."** Woody Mahony is a labor organizer who has feelings for Sharon. Francis Ford Coppola directed the 1968 film version, with 1960s pop star Petula Clark as Sharon and Fred Astaire as Finian.

FLOWER DRUM SONG

MUSIC: Richard Rodgers
LYRICS: Oscar Hammerstein II
BOOK: Oscar Hammerstein II and Joseph Fields
DIRECTOR: Gene Kelly
CHOREOGRAPHER: Carol Haney
OPENED: December 1, 1958, New York; a run of 600 performances

It was librettist Joseph Fields who first secured the rights to C.Y. Lee's novel and then approached Rodgers and Hammerstein to join him as collaborators. To dramatize the conflict between the traditional older Chinese-Americans living in San Francisco and their thoroughly Americanized offspring, the musical tells the story of Mei Li, a timid "picture bride" from China, who arrives to fulfill her contract to marry nightclub owner Sammy Fong. Sammy, however, prefers dancer Linda Low. The problem is resolved when Sammy's friend Wang Ta discovers that Mei Li really is the bride for him. Early in the show, Linda sings a bouncy tribute to the life of lipstick, lace, and flowers in **"I Enjoy Being a Girl."**

GODSPELL

MUSIC AND LYRICS: Stephen Schwartz
BOOK AND DIRECTION: John-Michael Tebelak
CHOREOGRAPHER: Michael Bennett
OPENED: May 5, 1971, New York; a run of 2,124 performances Off-Broadway, then 527 on Broadway

With its rock-flavored score, *Godspell* is a flower-child view of the Gospel of St. Matthew. Jesus, depicted as a clown-faced innocent with a Superman "S" on his shirt, leads a band of followers in dramatized parables, including the Prodigal Son, the Good Samaritan, the Pharisees, and the Tax Collector. After a parable on forgiveness, a follower of Jesus sings **"Day By Day."** The song would reach number thirteen in 1972 on the *Billboard* pop singles chart.

GREASE

MUSIC, LYRICS, AND BOOK: Jim Jacobs and Warren Casey
DIRECTOR: Tom Moore
CHOREOGRAPHER: Patricia Birch
OPENED: February 14, 1972, New York; a run of 3,388 performances

A surprise runaway hit reflecting the nostalgia fashion of the 1970s, *Grease* is the story of hip greaser Danny and his wholesome girl Sandy; a loose plot that serves as an excuse for the light-hearted ride through the early rock 'n' roll of the 1950s. The 1978 movie starring John Travolta and Olivia Newton-John, is one of the top-grossing musical movies of all time. At a sleepover, the girls talk about boys while trying cigarettes and alcohol. Marty reveals **"Freddy, My Love"** as a marine with whom she has a long-distance relationship. Tough girl Rizzo fears she might be pregnant. When consoled by chaste Sandy, Rizzo angrily lashes out at her, saying **"There Are Worse Things I Could Do."**

HAIRSPRAY

MUSIC: Marc Shaiman
LYRICS: Scott Wittman and Marc Shaiman
BOOK: Mark O'Donnell and Thomas Meehan
DIRECTOR: Jack O'Brien
CHOREOGRAPHER: Jerry Mitchell
OPENED: August 15, 2002, New York; a run of 2,642 performances

Film composer Marc Shaiman helped turn John Waters' campy 1988 movie *Hairspray* into perfect fodder for a new Broadway musical—teenage angst, racial integration, a lot of dancing, and a whole lot of hair. Plump heroine Tracy Turnblad dreams of dancing on the Corny Collins TV show, but is upstaged by the prettier, but less talented, current "It-girl" Amber Von Tussle. Tracy envisions good things for herself, as she knows she can take down Amber in **"I Can Hear the Bells."** Tracy eventually dances her way onto the Corny Collins TV show and gains acceptance for all teens of every size, shape, and color.

HANNAH MONTANA
(television)

MUSIC AND LYRICS: Matthew Gerard and Steve Diamond
DIRECTOR: Richard Correll, Barry O'Brien, Michael Poryes, et al.
FIRST BROADCAST: March 24, 2006, Disney Channel

The plot of the Disney Channel's successful television show is simple: Miley Stewart, played by Miley Cyrus is a typical teenage girl except that at night she becomes the teen pop sensation Hannah Montana. Miley learns to deal with the pressures facing the average teenager while experiencing the excitement and stress of fame. The show amassed a huge following, launching Cyrus onto music stages and the silver screen. One song she sings with her father (country music singer/songwriter/actor Billy Ray Cyrus) is "**I Learned from You.**" The song was adapted and used in the 2007 film *A Bridge to Terebithia*.

HERCULES
(film)

MUSIC AND LYRICS: Alan Menken and David Zippel
SCREENPLAY: Ron Clements, Donald McEnery, Bob Shaw, and Irene Mecchi
DIRECTORS: Ron Clements and John Musker
RLEASED: June 27, 1997, Walt Disney Pictures

Hercules marked Disney's return to the lighter musical comedy of its earlier animated musicals. In this snappy romp through Greek mythology, *Hercules* tells the story of the Greek hero, born of the gods but not quite immortal. As half man/half deity and all teenager, he tries to fit in, but it is painfully obvious to everyone, including himself that he does not and never will. Learning that he is the son of Zeus and must prove himself a "true hero" to regain his place among the deities, he enlists the help of a doting Pegasus and a satyr named Phil. Hercules becomes a famous hero, battling monsters, Hades, the Titans, and even saving Mt. Olympus, but in the end it is his love for Megara and his self-sacrifice to save her which makes him a true hero. Having regained his birthright, Hercules then gives it up to remain on earth with her. "**I Won't Say (I'm in Love)**" is the love song, sung by the stubborn Megara when she first has feelings for Hercules.

HIGH SCHOOL MUSICAL
(television)

MUSIC AND LYRICS: Matthew Gerrard, Robbie Nevil, Greg Cham, Ray Cham, Andrew Seeley, Andy Dodd, Adam Watts, David Lawrence, Faye Greenberg, Jamie Houston, Randy Petersen, and Kevin Quinn

SCREENPLAY: Peter Barsocchini
DIRECTOR: Kenny Ortega
AIRED: January 20, 2006, Walt Disney Pictures

The original Disney Channel movie *High School Musical* tells the story of Troy Bolton and Gabriella Montez, two high schoolers who discover their love for singing and challenge their cliques in the process. Due to record-breaking popularity, the television film was followed by two sequels: *High School Musical 2* (2007, television release) and *High School Musical 3: Senior Year* (2008, theatre release). Tony and Gabriella meet at a New Year's Eve party when they are called upon to sing at karaoke. They sing "**Start of Something New**" realizing their interest in each other. Back at school, the two attend the audition for the school musical but shyness and doubt keep them from following through. Sharpay and her brother Ryan step up and sing "**What I've Been Looking For.**" Having now summoned the courage to perform, Tony and Gabriella approach Ms. Darbus, the drama teacher, only to find the auditions closed. Darbus changes her mind and invites them to a callback after overhearing them sing while she was out of the room. Ms. Darbus gives them the lead roles in the musical.

INTO THE WOODS

MUSIC AND LYRICS: Stephen Sondheim
BOOK AND DIRECTION: James Lapine
CHOREOGRAPHER: Lar Lubovitch
OPENED: November 5, 1987, New York; a run of 765 performances

Into the Woods brought together for the second time the Pulitzer Prize winning team of Lapine and Sondheim. After their first collaboration, *Sunday in the Park with George*, this time they turned to children's fairy tales as their subject. The book of *Into the Woods* often focuses on the darker, grotesque aspects of these stories, but by highlighting them, it touches on themes of interpersonal relationships, death, and what we pass onto our children. Act I begins with the familiar "once upon a time" stories, and masterfully interweaves the plots of Snow White, Little Red Ridinghood, Cinderella, Jack and the Beanstalk, a Baker and his Wife, and others. Act II concerns what happens *after* "happily ever after," as reality sets in, and the fairy tales plots dissolve into the more human stories. Little Red Ridinghood sings the moral of her tale in **"I Know Things Now"** after disobeying her mother and ending up lunch to a hungry wolf.

JEKYLL & HYDE

MUSIC: Frank Wildhorn
LYRICS AND BOOK: Leslie Bricusse
DIRECTOR: Robin Phillips
CHOREOGRAPHER: Joey Pizzi
OPENED: April 28, 1997, New York; a run of 1,543 performances

The musical is based on Robert Louis Stevenson's 1886 novel *Dr. Jekyll and Mr. Hyde*. As in the book, a well-meaning scientist, Dr. Henry Jekyll, invents a potion that separates the noble side of man's nature from the evil, bestial side. Using himself as guinea pig, Jekyll soon finds he has unleashed an uncontrollable monster, Mr. Hyde, who cuts a murderous swath through London. Two women in his life help emphasize this difference: Jekyll's sweet innocent fiancée, Emma; and Hyde's scarlet-woman love, Lucy. Injured by a rough customer, Lucy finds herself being treated by the gentle Dr. Jekyll, and she fantasizes about a relationship with him in **"Someone Like You."**

LES MISÉRABLES

MUSIC: Claude-Michel Schönberg
LYRICS: Herbert Kretzmer and Alain Boublil
BOOK: Claude-Michel Schönberg and Alain Boublil
ORIGINAL FRENCH TEXT: Alain Boublil and Jean-Marc Natel
DIRECTORS: Trevor Nunn and John Caird
CHOREOGRAPHER: Kate Flatt
OPENED: September, 1980, Paris; an initial run of 3 months
        October 8, 1985, London
        March 12, 1987, New York; a run of 6,680 performances

This quasi-operatic pop epic was one of the defining musicals of the 1980s, distilling the drama from the 1,200 page Victor Hugo novel of social injustice and the plight of the downtrodden (the "miserable ones" of the title). The plot is too rich to encapsulate, but centers on Jean Valjean, a prisoner sentenced to years of hard labor for stealing a loaf of bread for his starving family. He escapes and tries to start a new life, but soon finds himself pursued by the relentless policeman Javert. The pursuit continues for years, across a tapestry of early 19th century France that includes an armed uprising against the government, in which Valjean takes a heroic part. Along the way he acquires an adopted daughter, Cosette, who grows into womanhood and attracts the attention of the handsome revolutionary Marius. As a girl working in an inn owned by the tyrannical Madame Thénardier, Cosette sings of the better life she longs for in **"Castle on a Cloud."** Much later, secretly in love with Marius, Eponine, a street waif, sings **"On My Own."**

THE LITTLE MERMAID

MUSIC: Alan Menken
LYRICS: Howard Ashman; additional Broadway lyrics by Glenn Slater
BOOK: Doug Wright
FILM DIRECTORS: John Musker and Ron Clements
FILM SCREENPLAY: John Musker and Ron Clements
FILM RELEASED: November 17, 1989, Walt Disney Pictures
BROADWAY DIRECTOR: Francesa Zambello
BROADWAY CHOREOGRAPHER: Stephen Mear
BROADWAY OPENING: January 10, 2008, New York; a run of 685 performances

Based on the Hans Christian Andersen tale, *The Little Mermaid* marked the Disney studio's triumphant return to the animated screen musical. Ariel, a young sea-dwelling mermaid, longs to be human. She falls in love with the human prince and, aided by some magic, gets her wish. **"Part of Your World"** is sung by Ariel as she observes human life from the water she cannot leave. The musical was adapted and expanded for the Broadway stage, with added songs.

A LITTLE PRINCESS

MUSIC: Andrew Lippa
LYRICS AND BOOK: Brian Crawley

A Little Princess, based on the novel by Frances Hodgson Burnett, is the story of a little girl with a great big imagination. Separated from her father and the open-hearted Africans who have helped him raise her, young Sara Crewe is sent to boarding school in London. When things go badly for her there, her imaginative powers come to the rescue helping to transform a drab institution into a place of magic and mystery. Sara sings **"Live Out Loud"** after the cruel headmistress Miss Minchin tries to squelch Sara's high spirits. As of this writing, the music has not opened in New York.

MULAN
(film)

MUSIC: Matthew Wilder
LYRICS: David Zippel
DIRECTORS: Tony Bancroft and Barry Cook
SCREENPLAY: Rita Hsiao, Chris Sanders, Philip LaZebnik, Raymond Singer, and Eugenia Bostwick-Singer
RELEASED: June 19, 1998, Walt Disney Pictures

Mulan is a retelling of a Chinese legend. The young woman Mulan disguises herself as her ailing father to take his place in mandated military service. Mulan's ancestors send the dragon Mushu to help as the woman risks her family's honor in saving China from the Hun army. **"Reflection"** is sung by Mulan when she realizes she does not fit the traditional definition of a "young bride" and wants to become the person she feels inside. The song was recorded by Christina Aguilera, hitting number 19 on the *Billboard* singles charts.

OKLAHOMA!

MUSIC: Richard Rodgers
LYRICS AND BOOK: Oscar Hammerstein II
DIRECTOR: Rouben Mamoulian
CHOREOGRAPHER: Agnes de Mille
OPENED: March 31, 1943, New York; a run of 2,212 performances

There are many reasons why *Oklahoma!* is a recognized landmark in the history of American musical theatre. In the initial collaboration between Richard Rodgers and Oscar Hammerstein II, it not only expertly fuses the major elements in the production—story, songs, and dance—it also utilizes dream ballets to reveal hidden desires and fears in the principal characters. In addition, the musical, based on Lynn Riggs' play, *Green Grow the Lilacs,* was the first with a book that honestly depicted the kind of rugged pioneers who had once tilled the land and tended the cattle. Set in Indian Territory soon after the turn of the century, *Oklahoma!* spins a simple tale mostly concerned with whether the decent Curly or the menacing Jud gets to take Laurey to the box social. A side story involves Ado Annie, an unsophisticated high-spirited ranch girl whose Pa has told Will Parker that if he comes up with $50 he can marry her. Will wins $50 in a rodeo in Kansas City. While he is away, Ado Annie agrees to go to the box social with peddler Ali Hakim. Attracted to both men, she sings of her predicament in **"I Cain't Say No."**

ONCE UPON A MATTRESS

MUSIC: Mary Rodgers
LYRICS: Marshall Barer
BOOK: Jay Thompson, Marshall Barer, and Dean Fuller
DIRECTOR: George Abbott
CHOREOGRAPHER: Joe Layton
OPENED: May 11, 1959, New York; a run of 2,214 performances

Once Upon a Mattress was first created as a one act musical by Mary Rodgers (daughter of Richard Rodgers) and Marshall Barer at an adult summer camp. They expanded the work, based on the fairy tale *The Princess and the Pea*, into a full evening's entertainment that was notable as the stage debut of Carol Burnett as Princess Winnifred. Queen Agravain has ruled that her son will only marry someone of royal blood. Winnifred spends a sleepless night, disturbed by one lone pea, planted by the queen, under a pile of mattresses. Actually, an accomplice has secretly stuffed the bed with an arsenal of uncomfortability. In **"Shy"** Princess Winnifred ironically introduces herself.

SMILE

MUSIC: Marvin Hamlisch
LYRICS, BOOK, AND DIRECTION: Howard Ashman
CHOREOGRAPHER: Mary Kyte
OPENED: November 24, 1986, New York; a run of 48 performances

The musical, a parody of beauty pageants, is based on the 1975 Jerry Belson film of the same name. The story follows two of the young hopefuls: Doria, a loser who hopes to transform her life, and Robin, who isn't quite sure how she got into all of this. Doria gives her motivation describing seeing her first pageant in **"Disneyland,"** an escape from reality.

THE SOUND OF MUSIC

MUSIC: Richard Rodgers
LYRICS: Oscar Hammerstein II
BOOK: Howard Lindsay and Russel Crouse
DIRECTOR: Vincent J. Donehue
CHOREOGRAPHER: Joe Layton
OPENED: November 16, 1959, New York; a run of 1,443 performances

The Sound of Music was adapted from Maria von Trapp's autobiographical *The Trapp Family Singers*. It is set in Austria in 1938 during the Anschluss (The Nazi annexation of Austria to Germany). Maria Rainer, a free-spirited postulant at Nonnburg Abbey takes a position as governess to the seven children of the widowed and autocratic Captain Georg von Trapp. Maria loosens things up around the house, which has been run like a battleship since the death of the children's mother, teaching the children to sing and play, and thereby melting the Captain's heart. After Maria and the Captain marry, the family flees over the Alps into Switzerland to escape the Nazis. In a flirtatious scene between Liesl (the Captain's eldest daughter) and Rolf (a young messenger), the couple hints at their feelings for each other singing **"Sixteen Going on Seventeen."**

SOUTH PACIFIC

MUSIC: Richard Rodgers
LYRICS: Oscar Hammerstein II
BOOK: Oscar Hammerstein II and Joshua Logan
DIRECTOR AND CHOREOGRAPHER: Joshua Logan
OPENED: April 7, 1949, New York; a run of 1,925 performances

On a U.S. Naval base in the south Pacific during World War II, an unlikely romance develops between Nellie Forbush, a naïve navy nurse from Little Rock, and Emile de Becoque, a sophisticated French planter living on the island. The musical is based on two short stories from *Tales of the South Pacific* by James Michener. For a follies revue show put on for the troops, Nellie gets into the spirit, dresses as a male sailor, and sings the raucous number **"Honey Bun"** to Luther Billis who is dressed as a hula-skirted native girl.

SPRING AWAKENING

MUSIC: Duncan Sheik
LYRICS AND BOOK: Steven Sater
DIRECTOR: Michael Mayer
CHOREOGRAPHER: Bill T. Jones
OPENED: December 10, 2006, New York; a run of 859 performances

This rock musical, 2007 Tony Award winner of Best Musical, is based on the 1891 German play by Frank Wedekind, which was banned for decades because of its frankness about teenage sex and suicide. The setting is a provincial German town in the 1890s. Teenagers struggle against strict morals of adults and the lack of instruction and communication about sex and emotion. Wendla Bergmann is a girl discovering her sexuality and sensuality in a time that forbids such things. She opens the show singing **"Mama Who Bore Me"** about all her mother has not told her.

13 — THE MUSICAL

MUSIC AND LYRICS: Jason Robert Brown
BOOK: Dan Elish and Robert Horn
DIRECTOR: Jeremy Sams
CHOREOGRAPHER: Christopher Gattelli
OPENED: October 5, 2008, New York; a run of 105 performances

Jason Robert Brown's *13* is a musical written for teenage singers. 13-year-old Evan Goldman finds out that, due to his parents divorce, he must move from New York City to Appleton, Indiana, with his mother. As if this weren't dreadful enough to a big city boy, Evan learns that he will be celebrating his Bar Mitzvah in Appleton, far away from all of his friends. He meets a quirky neighbor Patrice and she empathizes with his pitiable situation in **"The Lamest Place in the World."** Evan is soon confronted with having to choose his friends between the popular and cool clique of football star Brett, and unpopular Patrice. Evan snubs Patrice in favor of the cool crowd. Patrice is hurt and describes **"What It Means to Be a Friend"** to Archie who is trying to convince her to forgive.

TICK, TICK . . . BOOM!

MUSIC, LYRICS AND BOOK: Jonathan Larson
DIRECTOR: Scott Schwartz
CHOREOGRAPHER: Christopher Gattelli
OPENED: May 23, 2001, New York; closed January 6, 2002

Jonathan Larson, composer of *Rent*, struggled like many actors and writers in New York for years before he found success. After the unproduced *Superbia, tick, tick . . . BOOM!* was his second musical. Initially it was a one-man show that told Larson's autobiographical story about bohemian life in New York, which he performed himself at various times between 1989 and 1993. He lives on virtually nothing, passing up lucrative corporate job offers to follow his dream. Larson shelved it to spend time on *Rent*. After his death, interest in his earlier works emerged, and in 2001, *tick, tick . . . BOOM!* received a full Off-Broadway production, expanded to a three-character piece: Jonathan, his girlfriend Susan, and his best friend Michael. The show opens on a Saturday night in 1990, with Jonathan soon turning 30. Jonathan's musical *Superbia* is in workshop, and an actress in the show (the actor who plays Susan also play this character) sings **"Come to Your Senses,"** which is actually from Larson's unproduced show *Superbia*. After Micael reveals that he is HIV-positive, Jonathan contemplates their long friendship and the importance of every day as he faces his 30th birthday.

WICKED

MUSIC AND LYRICS: Stephen Schwartz
BOOK: Winnie Holzman
DIRECTOR: Joe Mantello
CHOREOGRAPHER: Wayne Cilento
OPENED: October 30, 2003

Based on Gregory Maguir's 1995 book, *Wicked* chronicles the back story of the Wicked Witch of the West, Elphaba, and Good Witch of the North, Glinda (Galinda), before their story threads are picked up in L. Frank Baum's *The Wonderful Wizard of Oz*. The two witches first cross paths in school as unlikely roommates. Elphaba, shy and green, learns from radiant Galinda just what it takes to be **"Popular."** Feeling unloved and left out, Elphaba pities herself in **"I'm Not That Girl."** In Emerald City the Wizard tricks Elphaba into using the Grimmerie (an ancient book of witch spells) to give Chistery, his monkey servant, the ability to fly. After she realizes that she has been used by the duplicitous Wizard, Elphaba runs off with the Grimmerie, being chased by the Wizard's palace guards. She is labeled "wicked" and casts a spell on a broomstick to make it fly. She flies off vowing to fight the Wizard in the song **"Defying Gravity."**

YOU'RE A GOOD MAN, CHARLIE BROWN

MUSIC, LYRICS, AND BOOK: Clark Gesner; Andrew Lippa added songs for the Broadway revival
DIRECTOR: Joseph Hardy
CHOREOGRAPHER: Patricia Birch
OPENED: March 7, 1967; a run of 1,597 performances

With Charles Schultz's appealing comic strip *Peanuts* as a general inspiration, Clark Gesner created a musical out of events in "a day made up of little moments picked from all the days of Charlie Brown, from Valentine's Day to the baseball season, from wild optimism to utter despair, all mixed with the lives of his friends (both human and non-human) and strung together on the string of a single day, from bright uncertain morning to hopeful starlit evening." Whew! For the 1997 Broadway revival, Andrew Lippa wrote two new numbers, including, **"My New Philosophy"** for Sally, which becomes the standout number of the show. Sally has just received a D- at school, and is struggling to bounce back.

I GOT THE SUN IN THE MORNING
from the Stage Production *Annie Get Your Gun*

Words and Music by
IRVING BERLIN

Allegro moderato

ANNIE:

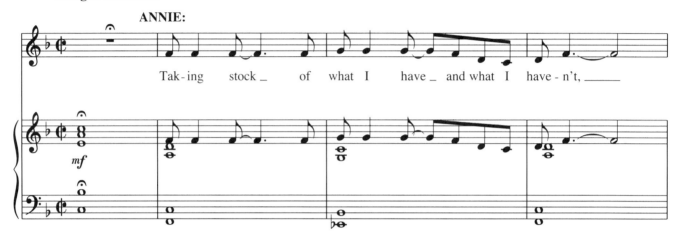

Tak-ing stock _ of what I have _ and what I have-n't, _____

What do I find? _ The things I have will keep me sat-is-fied. _____

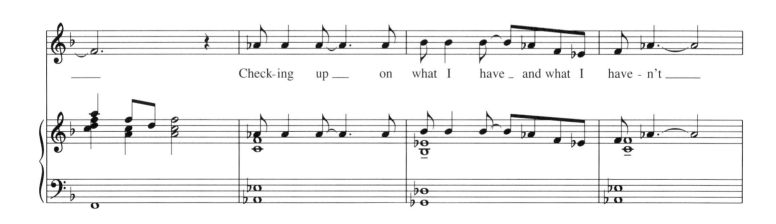

_____ Check-ing up _ on what I have _ and what I have-n't _____

What do I find? __ A health-y bal-ance on the cred-it side. _____

Bounce (♫ = ♩♪)

Got no dia - mond, got no pearl, __ Still I think __ I'm a
Got no but - ler, got no maid, __ Still I think __ I've been

luck - y girl, __ I got the sun in the morn-ing and the moon at night. _____
o - ver paid, __ I got the sun in the morn-ing and the moon at night. _____

Got no man - sion, got no yacht, __
Got no sil - ver, got no gold, __

A CHANGE IN ME

from Walt Disney's *Beauty and the Beast: The Broadway Musical*

Words by TIM RICE
Music by ALAN MENKEN

For now I love the world I see. _____

No change of heart, a change in me. _____

For in my dark de- spair

I slow - ly un - der-stood. My per - fect world out there

MEMORY
from *Cats*

Music by ANDREW LLOYD WEBBER
Text by TREVOR NUNN after T.S. ELIOT

Day - light.___ I must wait for the sun - rise,___ I must think of a new life___ and I must-n't give

in.___ When the dawn comes tonight will be a mem-o-ry too___ and a

new day___ will be - gin.

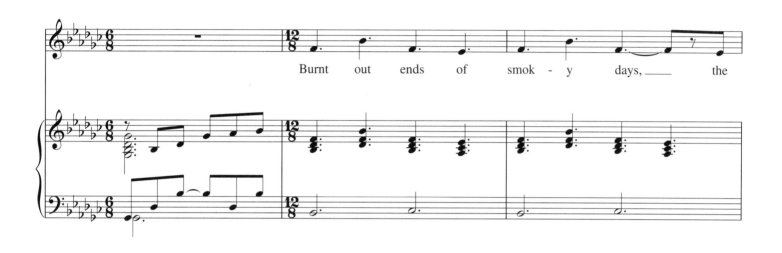

Burnt out ends of smok - y days, _____ the

stale cold smell __ of morn - ing. _____ The street lamp dies, an - oth - er

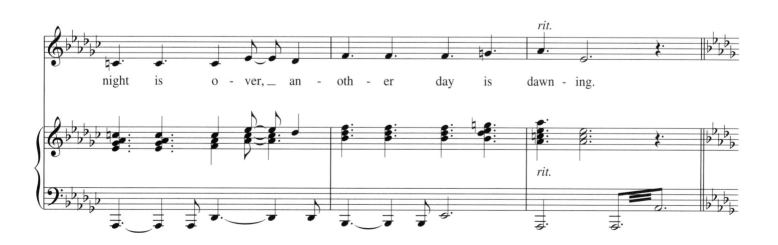

night is o - ver, __ an - oth - er day is dawn - ing.

rit.

Touch me. It's so eas-y to leave me all a - lone with the

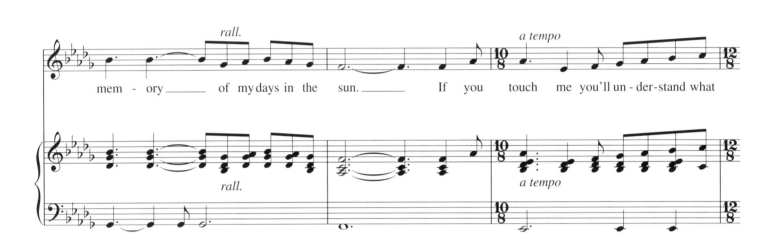

mem - ory of my days in the sun. If you touch me you'll un - der-stand what

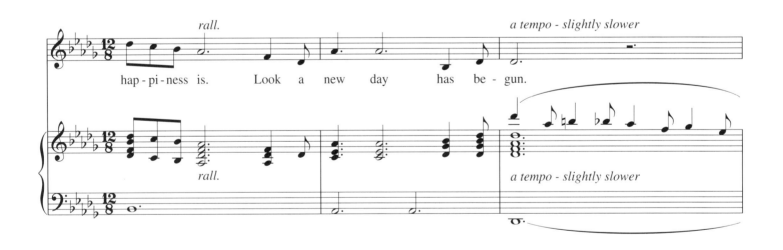

hap - pi - ness is. Look a new day has be - gun.

IN MY OWN LITTLE CORNER

from *Cinderella*

Lyrics by OSCAR HAMMERSTEIN II
Music by RICHARD RODGERS

CINDERELLA:

I'm as mild and as meek as a

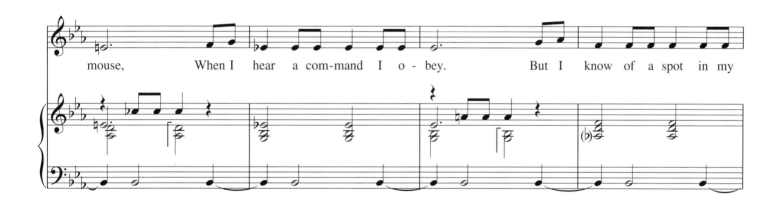

mouse, When I hear a com-mand I o - bey. But I know of a spot in my

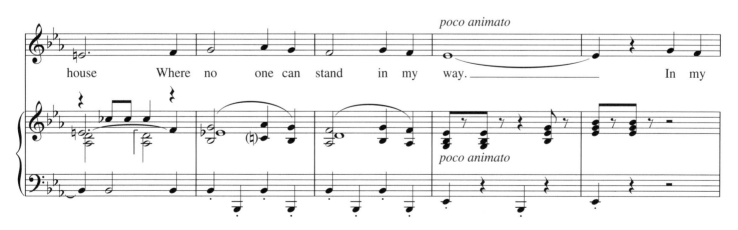

house Where no one can stand in my way. _____ In my

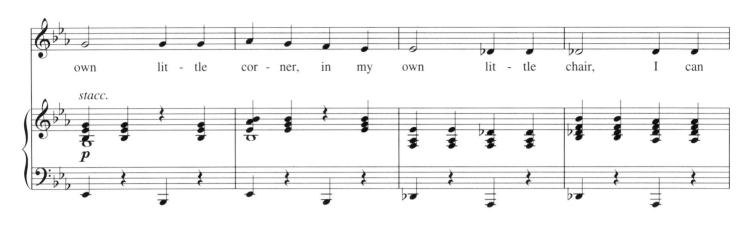

own lit - tle cor - ner, in my own lit - tle chair, I can

be what - ev - er I want to be. _____ On the

wing of my fan - cy I can fly an - y - where And the

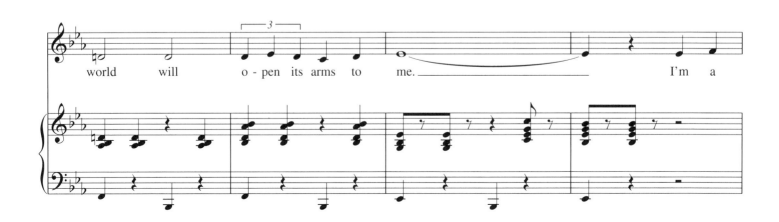

world will o - pen its arms to me. _____ I'm a

young Nor - we - gian prin - cess or a milk maid, _____ I'm the

great - est pri - ma don - na in Mi - lan, _____ I'm an

heir - ess who has al - ways had her silk made _____ By her

own flock of silk - worms in Ja - pan! _____ I'm a

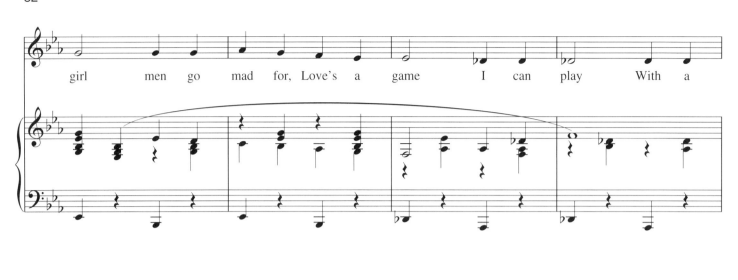

girl men go mad for, Love's a game I can play With a

cool and con - fi - dent kind of air, _____ Just as

long as I stay in my own lit - tle cor - ner, _____ All a -

lone in my own lit - tle chair.

hunt - ress on an Af - ri - can sa - fa - ri _____ (It's a

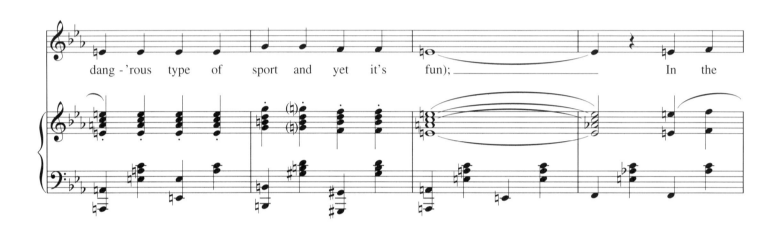

dang -'rous type of sport and yet it's fun); _____ In the

night I sal - ly forth to seek my quar - ry, _____ And I

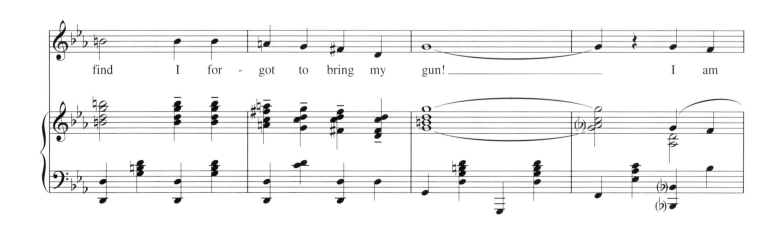

find I for - got to bring my gun! _____ I am

STEPSISTERS' LAMENT

from *Cinderella*

Lyrics by OSCAR HAMMERSTEIN II
Music by RICHARD RODGERS

Why would a fel-low want a girl like her, a frail and fluf-fy beau - ty?

Why can't a fel-low ev - er once pre-fer a sol - id girl like me? She's a froth-y lit-tle

In the show this song is sung by both sisters.

cheeks are a pret-ty shade of pink, But not an-y pink-er than a rose is. Her

skin may be del-i-cate and soft, But not an-y soft-er than a doe's is. Her

neck is no whit-er than a swan's. She's on-ly as dain-ty as a dai-sy. She's

on-ly as grace-ful as a bird. So why is the fel-low go-ing cra-zy? Oh,

39

WHAT I DID FOR LOVE

from *A Chorus Line*

Music by MARVIN HAMLISCH
Lyric by EDWARD KLEBAN

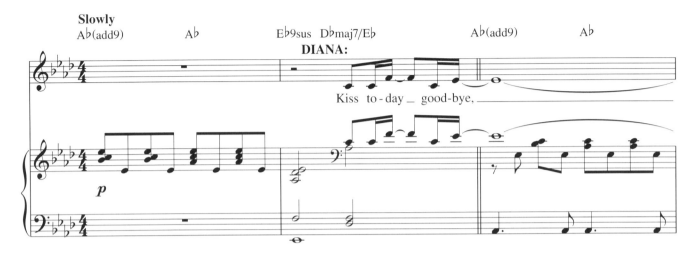

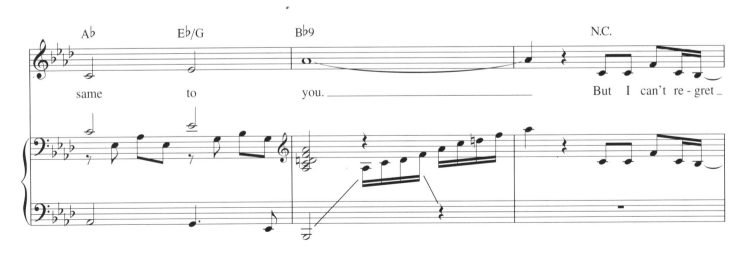

HOW ARE THINGS IN GLOCCA MORRA

from *Finian's Rainbow*

Words by E.Y. "Yip" HARBURG
Music by BURTON LANE

Lento espress.

please _____ How are things in Gloc-ca Mor - ra? _____ Is that lit-tle brook still

p espressivo   *colla voce*

leap-ing there? _____ Does it still run down to Don-ny Cove? _____ Through

Kil-ly-begs, _____ Kil-ker-ry and Kil-dare? _____ How are things in Gloc-ca

Mor-ra? _____ Is that wil-low tree still weep-ing there? _____ Does that lad-die with the

twin-klin' eye _____ Come whist-lin' by _____ And does he walk a-way sad and

dream-y there _____ not to see me there? _____ So I

ask each weep-ing wil-low, And each brook a-long the way, And each

lad that comes a-whist-lin' 'Too-ra-lay.' _____ How are

I ENJOY BEING A GIRL
from *Flower Drum Song*

Lyrics by OSCAR HAMMERSTEIN II
Music by RICHARD RODGERS

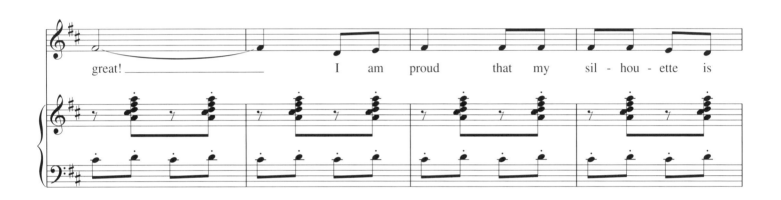

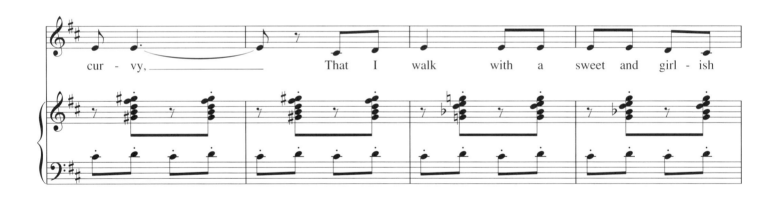

swerv-y._____ I a - dore be - ing dressed in some-thing fril - ly _____ When my

date comes to get me at my place. Out I go with my Joe or John or Bil - ly, _____ Like a

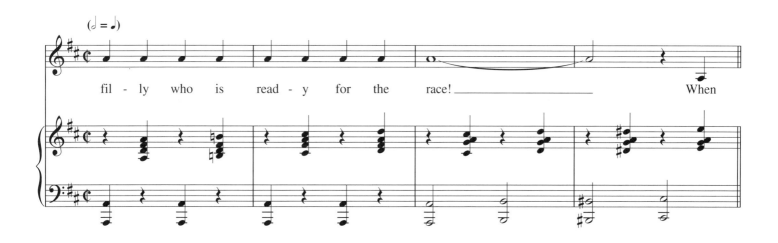

fil - ly who is read - y for the race! _____ When

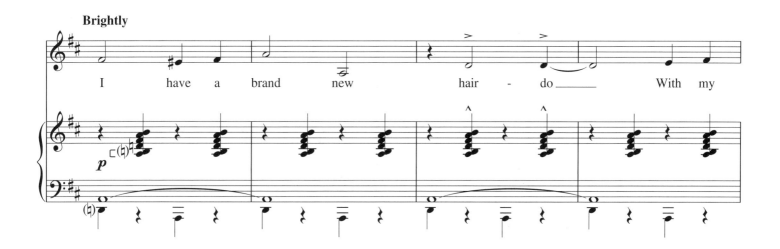

I have a brand new hair - do _____ With my

teeth are-n't teeth but pearl, _____ I

just lap it up like hon - ey, _____ I en -

joy be - ing a girl. _____ I

flip when a fel - low sends me flow - ers, _____ I

drool o - ver dress - es made of lace._____ I

talk on the tel - e - phone for ho - urs_____ With a

pound and a half of cream up - on my face._____ I'm
8va
f   *p*

strict - ly a fe - male fe - male____ And my

53

me. _____ When

men say I'm sweet as can - dy, _____ As a -

round in a dance we whirl, _____ It

goes to my head like bran - dy, _____ I en -

When I hear the com - pli - men - t'ry whis - tle _____ That

greets my bi - ki - ni by the sea, _____ I turn and I

glow - er and I bris - tle, _____ But I'm hap - py to know the whis-tle's meant for

me! _____ I'm strict - ly a fe - male fe - male ____

DAY BY DAY
from the Musical *Godspell*

Music by STEPHEN SCHWARTZ
Lyrics by RICHARD OF CHICHESTER (1197-1253)

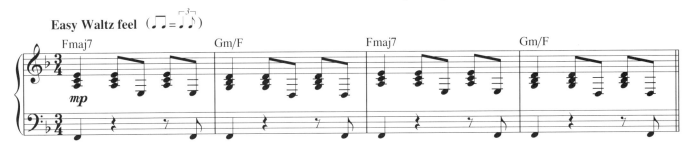

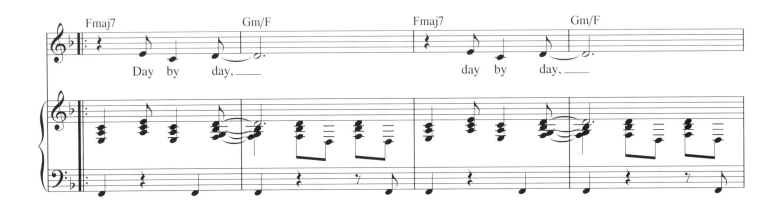

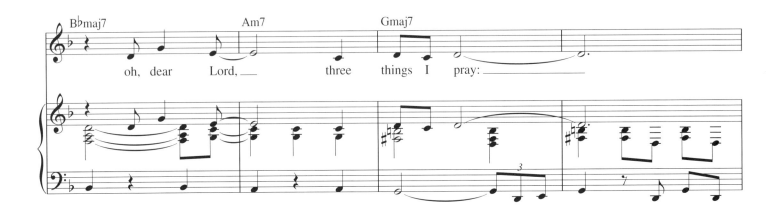

FREDDY, MY LOVE

from *Grease*

Lyric and Music by WARREN CASEY
and JIM JACOBS

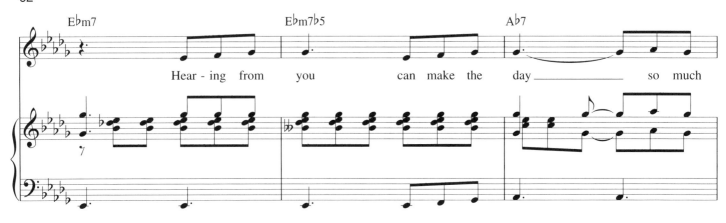

Hear-ing from you can make the day _____ so much

bet - ter, __ get-ting a sou - ve - nir or may - be a

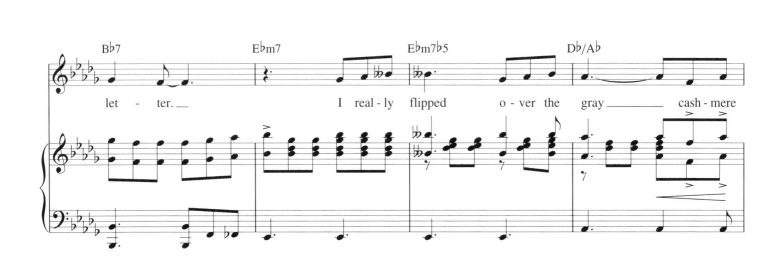

let - ter. __ I real-ly flipped o - ver the gray _____ cash-mere

sweat - er, Fred-dy, my love, Fred-dy, my love, Fred-dy, my love, Fred-dy, my

hon - ey,___ so is mine. I trea - sure___ ev - 'ry gift - ie,___ the

ring is___ real - ly nift - y,___ you say it___ cost you

fif - ty,___ so you're thrift - y,___ I don't mind, oohh,___ oh! Fred - dy, you'll

see, you'll hold me in your___ arms some day; and I will

THERE ARE WORSE THINGS I COULD DO

from *Grease*

Lyric and Music by WARREN CASEY
and JIM JACOBS

I CAN HEAR THE BELLS

from *Hairspray*

Music by MARC SHAIMAN
Lyrics by MARC SHAIMAN and SCOTT WITTMAN

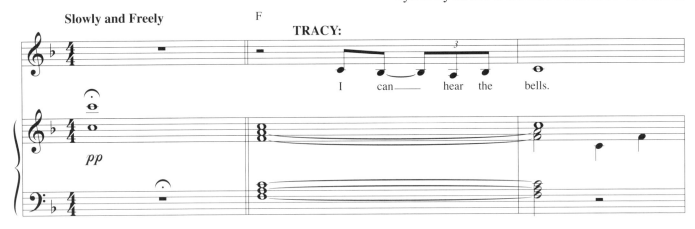

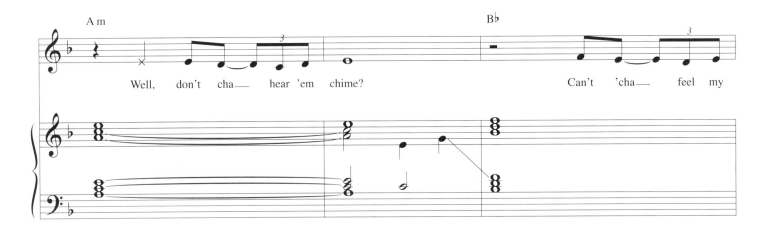

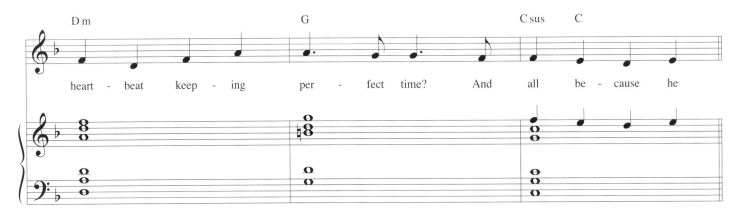

walks me down the aisle._____ My moth-er starts to cry, but I can't see 'cause Link and I are French -

kiss - in'. Lis - ten! I can__ hear the bells._____

I can__ hear the bells. My head is reel - in'. I can__ hear the bells. I

* Optional ending

I WON'T SAY
(I'M IN LOVE)
from Walt Disney Pictures' *Hercules*

Music by ALAN MENKEN
Lyrics by DAVID ZIPPEL

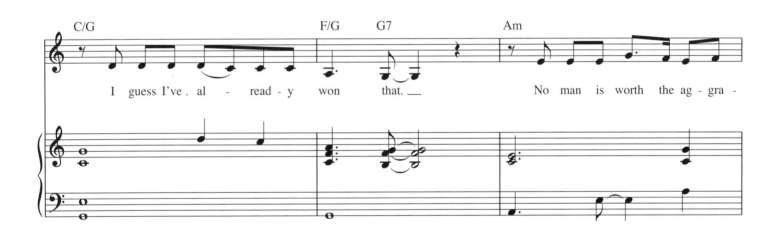

I LEARNED FROM YOU
from the Television Show *Hannah Montana*

Words and Music by MATTHEW GERRARD
and STEVE DIAMOND

Moderately slow, in 1

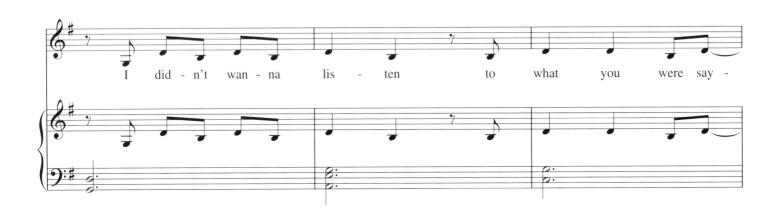

I did-n't wan-na lis-ten to what you were say-

-ing. I thought that I____ knew all I need to know.____

This duet has been adapted as a solo for this edition.

ques - tion.   That's   a   les - son   that   I   learned   from

you. _____

You   taught   me   to   stand____   on   my____   own,   and   I

thank you for that.____ It saved me, it made me.

And now that I'm ____ look - ing back ____ I can

say, ____ whoa. ____

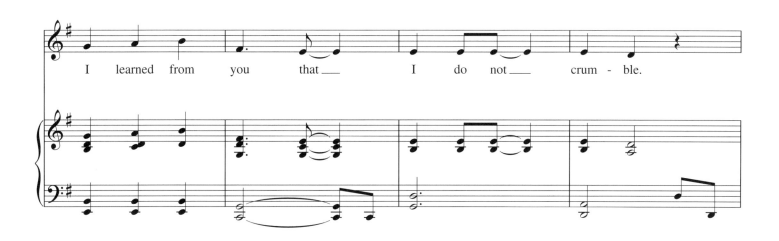

I learned from you that ___ I do not ___ crum - ble.

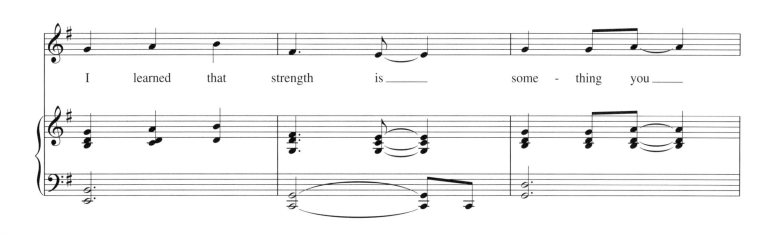

I learned that strength is ____ some - thing you ___

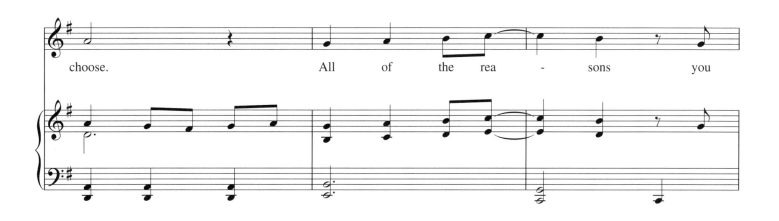

choose. All of the rea - sons you

keep on be - liev - ing, there's no

ques - tion: that's a les - son that I learned from

you. _____

I learned that strength is ___ some - thing you ___

choose. All of the rea - sons you keep on be - liev - ing,

there's no ques - tion: that's a les - son I learned from

you, _____ I learned from

you. _____

I KNOW THINGS NOW

from *Into the Woods*

Words and Music by
STEPHEN SONDHEIM

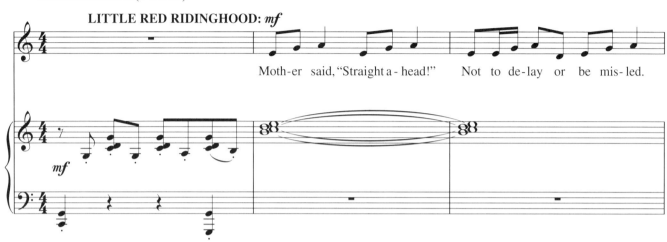

way that they should. And take ex - tra care with stran - gers, E - ven flow - ers have their dan - gers. And though

scar - y is ex - cit - ing, Nice is dif-f'rent than good.

Now I know: don't be scared. Gran - ny is right, just be pre - pared. Is - n't it nice to know a lot!

And a lit - tle bit not...

START OF SOMETHING NEW

from the Disney Channel Original Movie *High School Musical*

Words and Music by MATTHEW GERRARD
and ROBBIE NEVIL

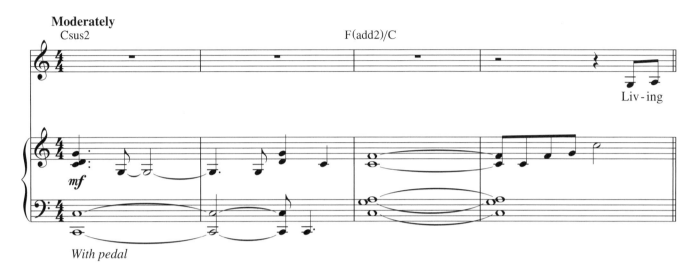

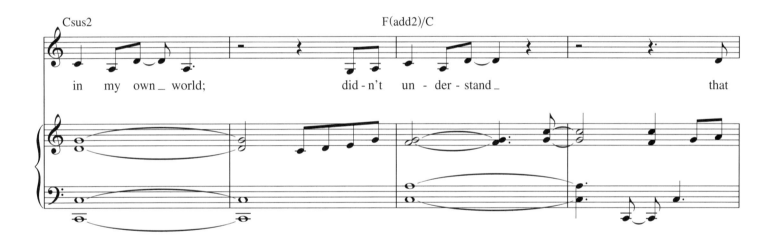

Originally a duet, this song has been adapted for this solo edition.

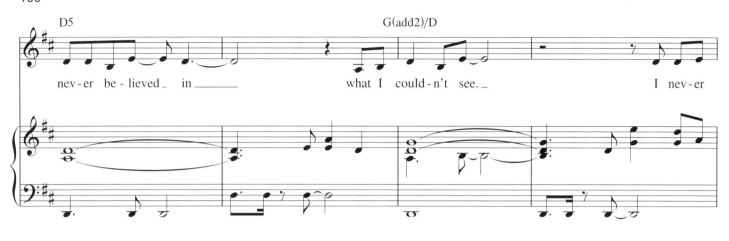

nev-er be-lieved _ in _____ what I could-n't see. _ I nev-er

o-pened my heart _ to all the pos-si-bil-i-ties. _ Oh, _ I

know that some-thing has changed; _ nev-er felt this way. ___ And right here to-night, _
I know it for real: _

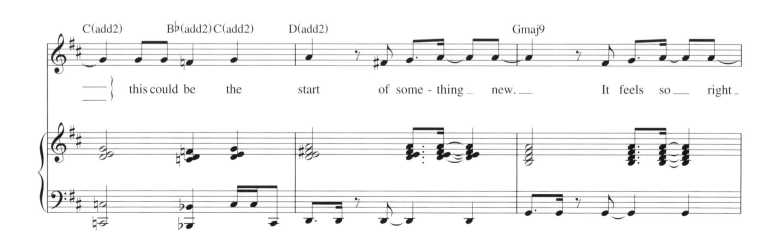

this could be the start of some-thing _ new. _ It feels so ___ right _

looks so much bright - er, oh, __ with you by my __ side. _____

D.S. al Coda   **CODA**

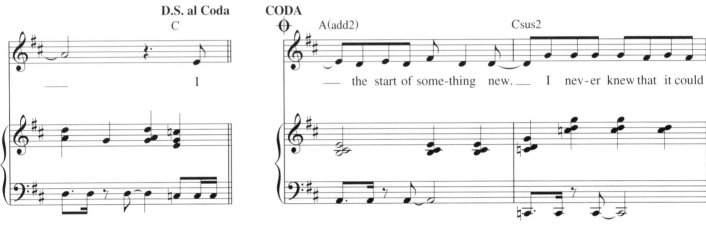

__ the start of some-thing new. __ I nev-er knew that it could

hap-pen till it hap-pened to me. ___ Oh, _____ yeah. _____

I did-n't know it be - fore, ___ but now it's eas-y to see, _____ oh. ___

WHAT I'VE BEEN LOOKING FOR

from the Disney Channel Original Movie *High School Musical*

Words and Music by ANDY DODD
and ADAM WATTS

It's hard to be - lieve ___ that I could-n't see ___ you were

al - ways there be - side me. ___ Thought I was a - lone, ___ with no one to hold; ___

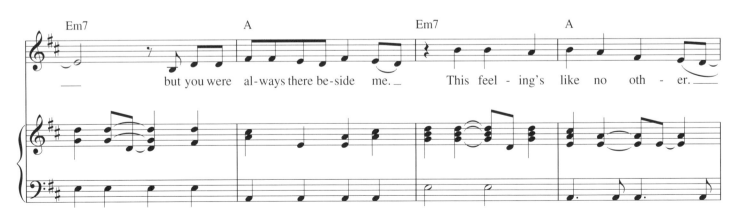

but you were al-ways there be-side me. ___ This feel - ing's like no oth - er. ___

Originally a duet, this song has been adapted for this solo edition.

I've been look-ing for. _____

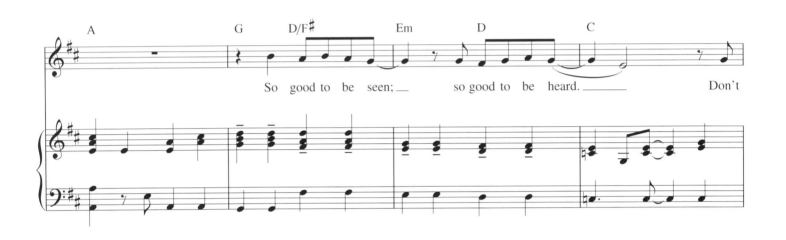

So good to be seen; ___ so good to be heard. _____ Don't

have to say a word. _____ For so long, I was lost; ___ so good to be found. _

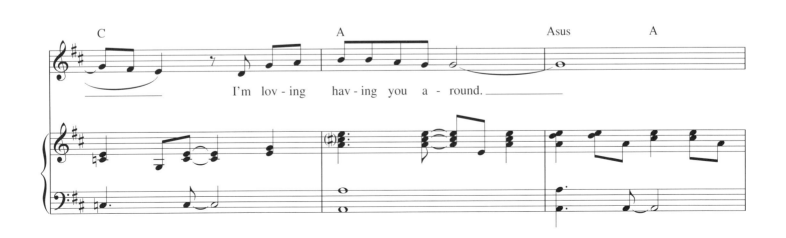

_____ I'm lov-ing hav-ing you a-round. _____

SOMEONE LIKE YOU
from the Broadway Musical *Jekyll & Hyde*

Words by LESLIE BRICUSSE
Music by FRANK WILDHORN

CASTLE ON A CLOUD
from *Les Misérables*

Music by CLAUDE-MICHEL SCHÖNBERG
Lyrics by ALAIN BOUBLIL, JEAN MARC NATEL
and HERBERT KRETZMER

COSETTE:

There is a cas - tle on a cloud.
There is a room that's full of toys.

I like to go there in my sleep.
There are a hun - dred boys and girls.

ON MY OWN
from *Les Misérables*

Music by CLAUDE-MICHEL SCHÖNBERG
Lyrics by ALAIN BOUBLIL, JEAN-MARC NATEL,
HERBERT KRETZMER, JOHN CAIRD and TREVOR NUNN

EPONINE:

And now I'm all a-lone a-gain, no-where to go, no one to turn to.

I did not want your mon-ey sir, I came out here 'cos I was told to, And now the night is

near, Now I can make be - lieve he's here.

Some-times I walk a-lone at night when ev-ery-bod-y else is sleep - ing,

I think of him and then I'm hap-py with the com-pa-ny I'm keep - ing. The ci - ty goes to

round me. And when I lose my way I close my eyes and he has
star - light. And all I see is him and me for - ev - er and for -

Più mosso

found me. In the know it's on - ly in my
ev - er. And I

mind That I'm talk - ing to my - self and not to him. And al -

though I know that he is blind, Still I say there's a way for us. I

love him, _____ but when the night is o - ver _____ he is

gone, the riv - er's just a riv - er. With -

out him the world a - round me chang - es. The

trees are bare and ev - 'ry-where the streets are full of strang - ers. I

PART OF YOUR WORLD
from Walt Disney's *The Little Mermaid - A Broadway Musical*

Music by ALAN MENKEN
Lyrics by HOWARD ASHMAN

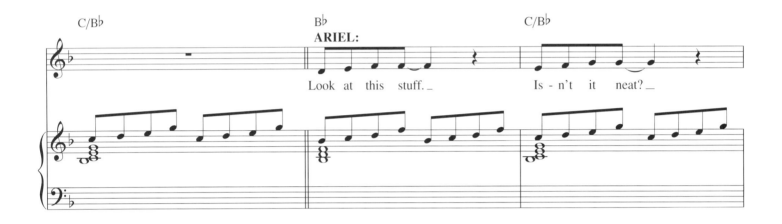

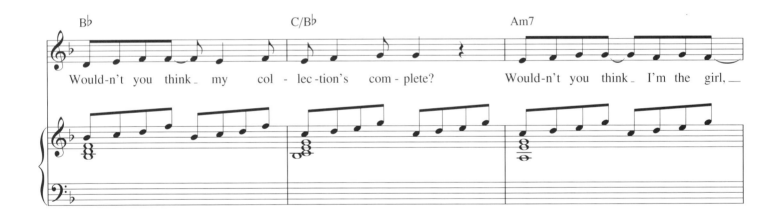

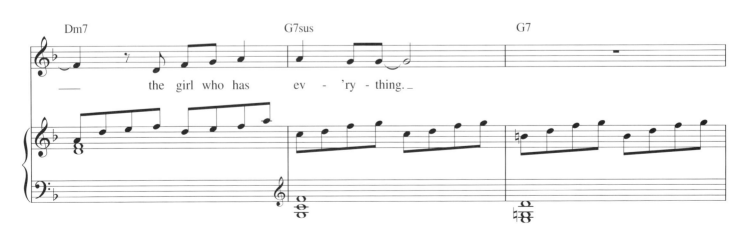

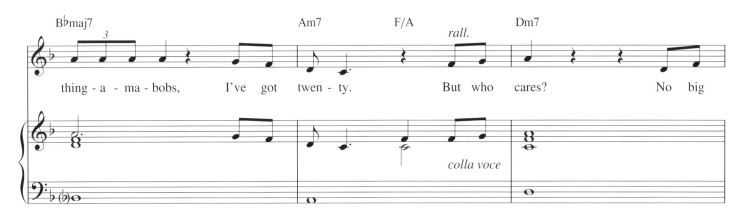

thing - a - ma - bobs, I've got twen - ty. But who cares? No big

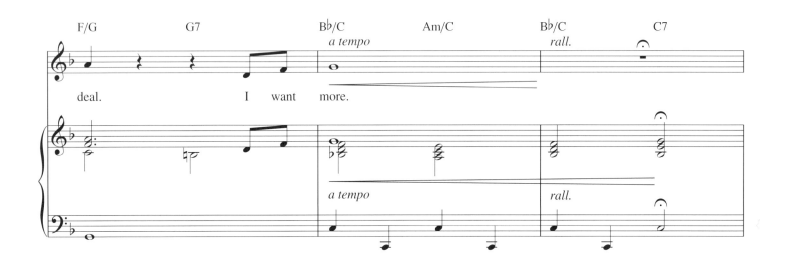

deal. I want more.

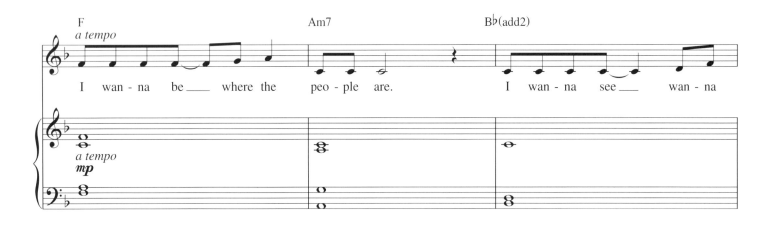

I wan - na be ___ where the peo - ple are. I wan - na see ___ wan - na

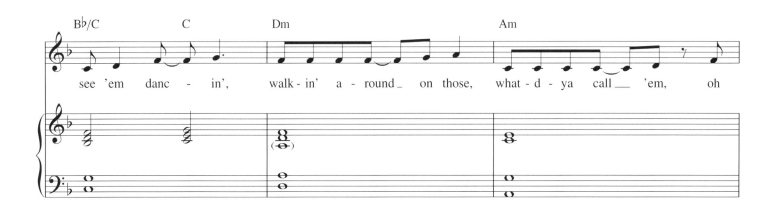

see 'em danc - in', walk - in' a - round ___ on those, what - d - ya call ___ 'em, oh

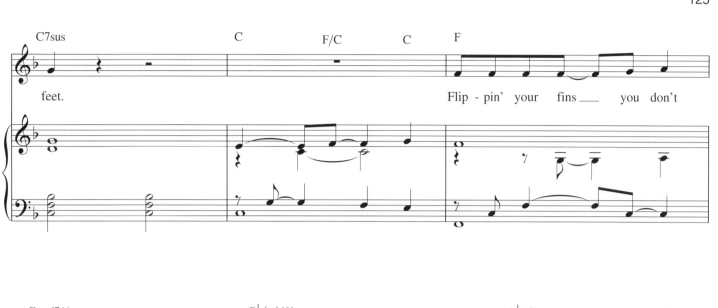

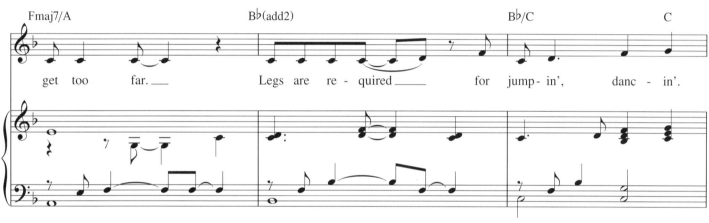

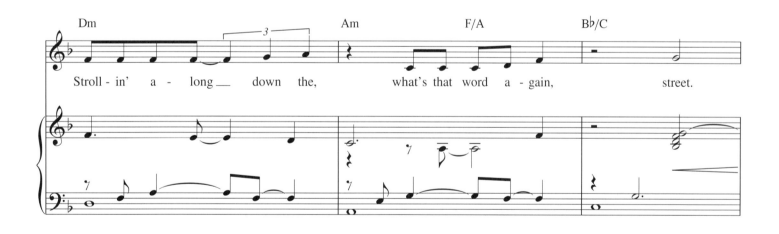

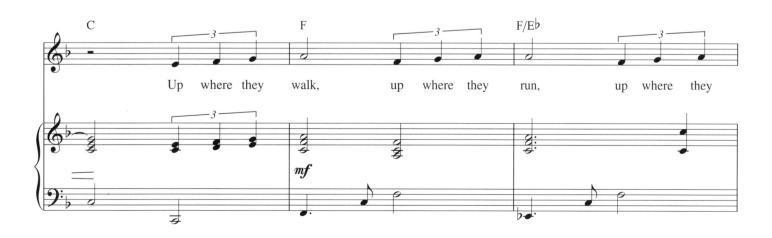

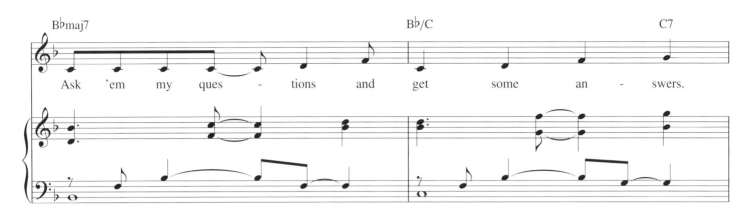

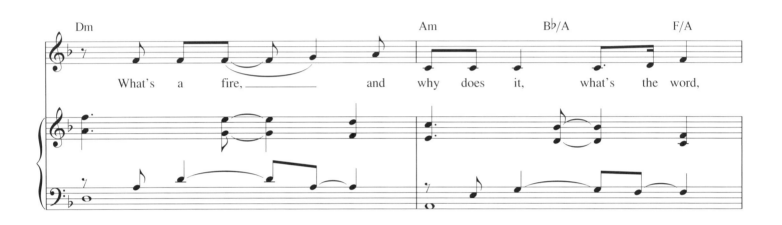

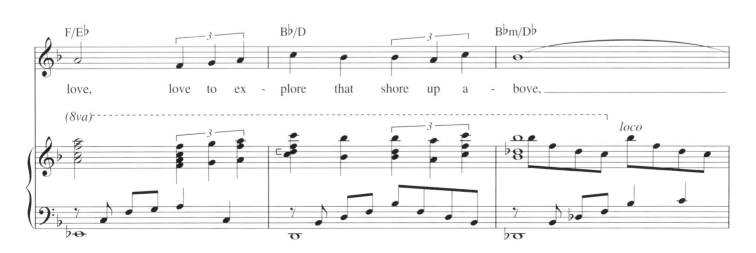

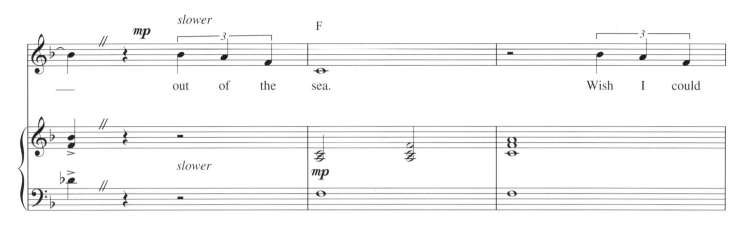

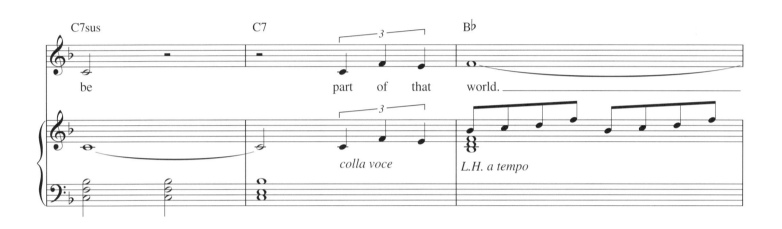

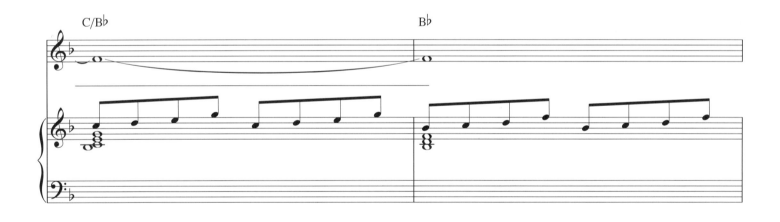

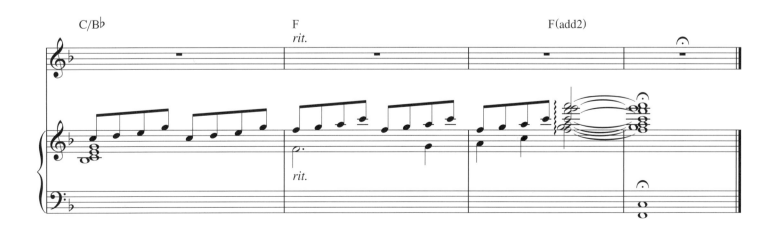

LIVE OUT LOUD
from *A Little Princess*

Music by ANDREW LIPPA
Lyrics by BRIAN CRAWLEY

Gentle, but with a strong sense of time

133

134

Quasi African Drums

I want the life they took a - way from me!

If that makes__ me head - strong,__ fine. That's a fault__ I'm glad__

__ is mine.__ I don't want to go__ a - long__ with the crowd.__

__ Don't want my spir - it bro - ken and bowed.__ Why do I have__

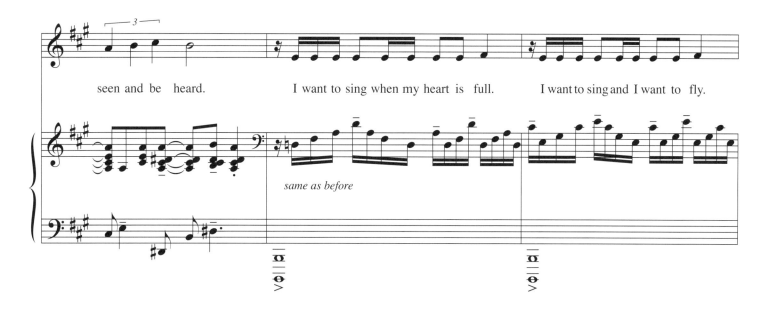

seen and be heard.   I want to sing when my heart is full.   I want to sing and I want to fly.

same as before

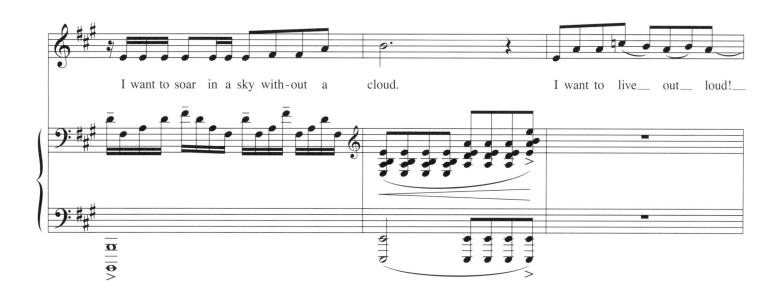

I want to soar in a sky with-out a   cloud.   I want to live__ out__ loud!__

ff

REFLECTION
from Walt Disney Pictures' *Mulan*

Music by MATTHEW WILDER
Lyrics by DAVID ZIPPEL

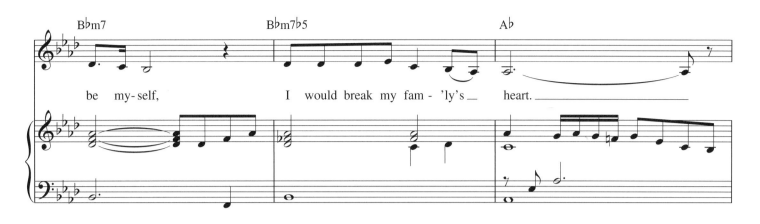

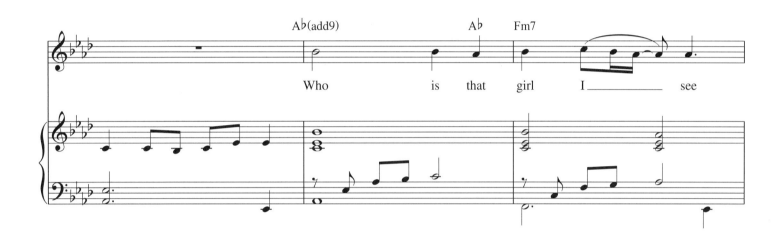

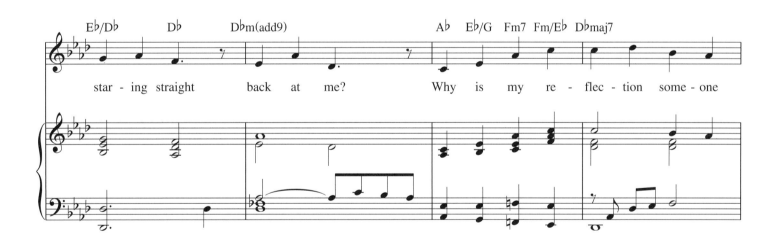

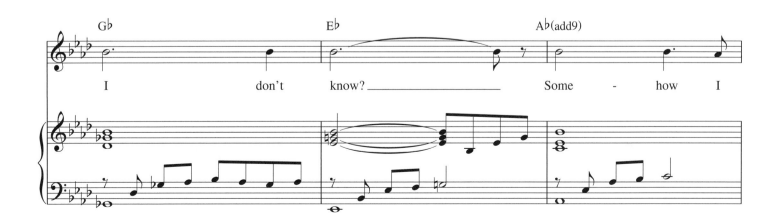

I CAIN'T SAY NO

from *Oklahoma!*

Lyrics by OSCAR HAMMERSTEIN II
Music by RICHARD RODGERS

Moderately
ADO ANNIE:

It ain't so much a ques-tion of not know-in' whut to do, I

knowed whut's right and wrong since I been ten. I

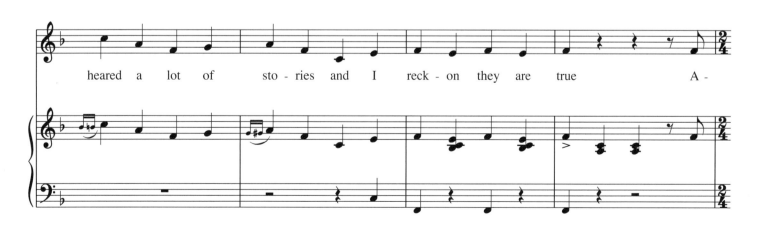

heared a lot of sto-ries and I reck-on they are true A-

142

bout how girls 're put up-on by men.   I

know I mus-n't fall in-to the pit, _____ But when I'm with a fel-ler, I fer -

git!

I'm jist a girl who cain't say no,
I'm jist a girl who cain't say no,

know she or - ta give his face a smack. _____ But as
set - tin' on the vel - ve - teen set - tee _____ 'Nen I

soon as some - one kiss - es me, I
think of thet ol' gold - en rule, And

some - how sort - a want - a kiss him back! _____
do fer him whut he would do him fer me! _____

I'm jist a fool when lights are low,
I caint re - sist a Ro - me - o,

146

sweet - er 'n cream and he's got - ta have cream or

die? Whut you goin' to do when he

talks thet way? Spit in his eye?

D.S. al Coda

CODA

SHY
from *Once Upon a Mattress*

Words by MARSHALL BARER
Music by MARY RODGERS

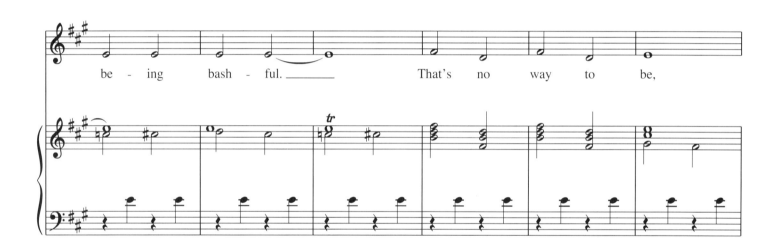

And you may be sure: _____ way down deep I'm de-

mure. _____ Though some peo-ple I know might de-ny it, At

bot-tom I'm qui-et and pure! _____ I'm a-ware that it's

wrong ___ to be meek as I am; My chanc-es may pass me by. I pre-tend to be

strong_____ but as weak as I am, All I can do is try. God knows I

try! _____ Though I'm fright-ened and shy _____

_____ And de - spite the im - pres - sion I give, I con - fess that I'm liv - ing a

Rubato

lie, _____ Be - cause I'm ac - tual - ly ter - ri - bly ti - mid and hor - ri - bly

Moderate 2

shy. _____ Though a

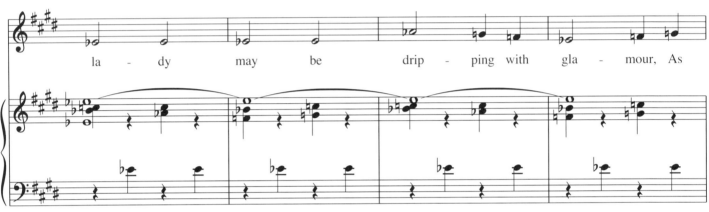

la - dy may be drip - ping with gla - mour, As

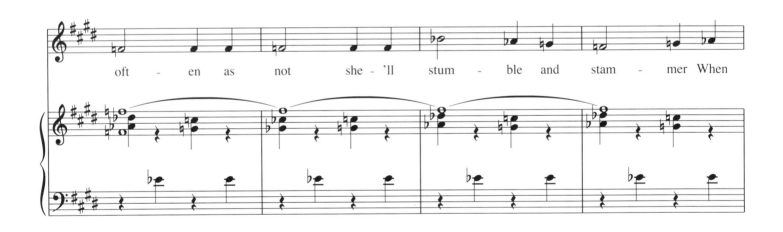

oft - en as not she 'll stum - ble and stam - mer When

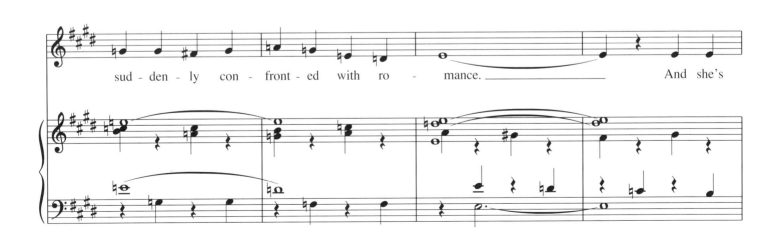

sud - den - ly con - front - ed with ro - mance. _____ And she's

like - ly to fall on her face _____ When she's

fi - nal-ly face to face with a pair of pants.

Quite oft - en the la - dy's not as

hard to please as she seems. _____ Quite

154

But how much long - er must I wait With

bait - ed breath and ho - ok? And that is

why, _____ Though I'm pain-ful-ly shy, _____ I'm in-sane to know

Più mosso - Charleston beat

Which sir? _____ You, sir _____ Not you, sir. _____ Then who, sir? _____

DISNEYLAND
from *Smile*

Words by HOWARD ASHMAN
Music by MARVIN HAMLISCH

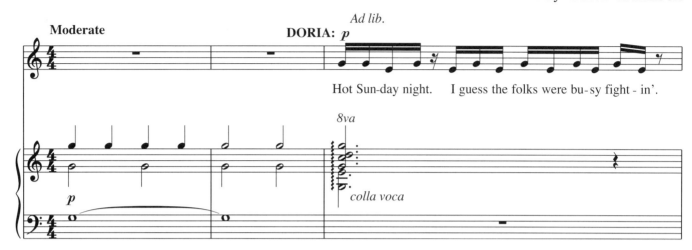

down on state nine-ty - three,__ so I'd sit thru the night_ by our old_ black-and-white_ T.

V.____ And that's where I saw it, that's when I

heard it _____ call - in',

call - in' me. _____

Dis - ney-land _ on a west - ern breeze, mag - ic car - pet,

please, car - ry me a - way _

Oh, I know you're gon-na say the trees are pa-per-mâc-hé, _ It's done with

solo

mir - rors, the mag - ic there. _ Each lit - tle bird's full of springs, _ you press a but-ton, it sings, _ re-cord-ed

mu - sic in the air.___ They've had the moun - tain re - faced,__ it's on - ly ply-wood and paste.__ Go on,__

___ *SAY IT!* I'll turn a - round __ and tell you, I don't

care!_____ I don't

care. I will live in _____ Dis - ney - land,

take me there __ to Dis - ney - land, _____

__ and when I get to Dis - ney - land

I'll stay. _____

Slow

SIXTEEN GOING ON SEVENTEEN

from *The Sound of Music*

Lyrics by OSCAR HAMMERSTEIN II
Music by RICHARD RODGERS

scared am I of things be - yond my ken.

I need some - one old - er and wis - er Tell - ing me what to

do. _____ You are sev - en - teen, go - ing on eight - een,

I'll ____ de - pend ___ on you. _____

MAMA WHO BORE ME

from *Spring Awakening*

Music by DUNCAN SHEIK
Lyrics by STEVEN SATER

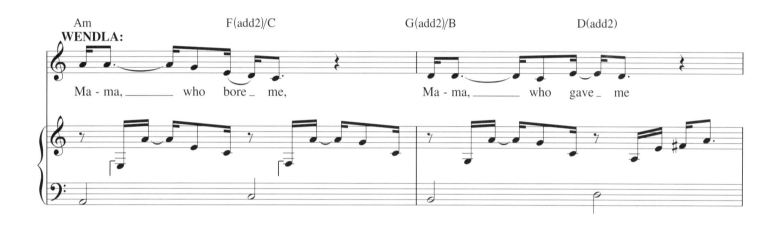

Ma - ma, who bore me, Ma - ma, who gave me

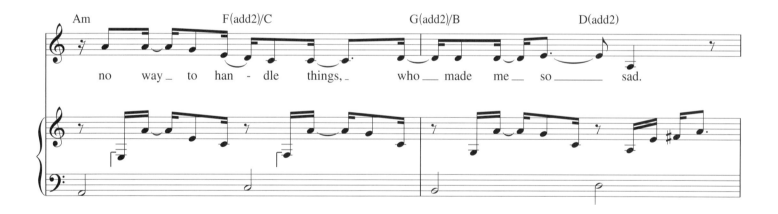

no way to han - dle things, who made me so sad.

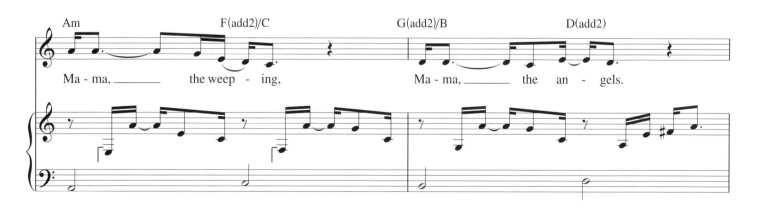

Ma - ma, the weep - ing, Ma - ma, the an - gels.

No sleep _ inHeav - en or Beth - le - hem. _ Some pray that _ one day _ Christ _

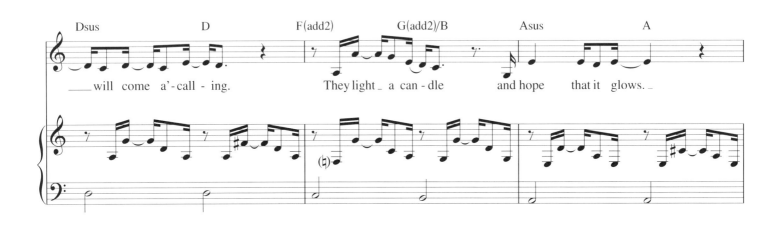

___ will come a'- call - ing. They light _ a can - dle and hope that it glows. _

And some _ just lie _ there, cry - ing for him to come _ and find _ them. But

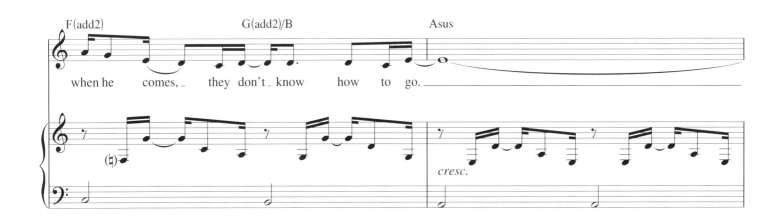

when he comes, _ they don't _ know how to go. _____

HONEY BUN
from *South Pacific*

Lyrics by OSCAR HAMMERSTEIN II
Music by RICHARD RODGERS

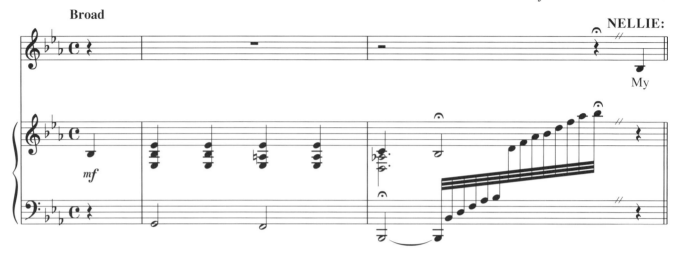

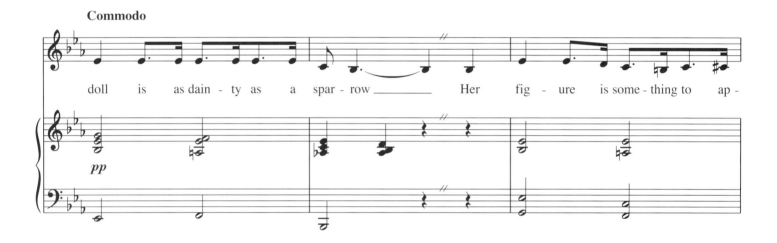

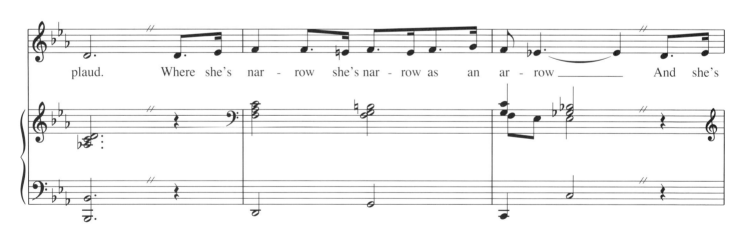

172

THE LAMEST PLACE IN THE WORLD
from the Broadway Musical *13*

Music and Lyrics by
JASON ROBERT BROWN

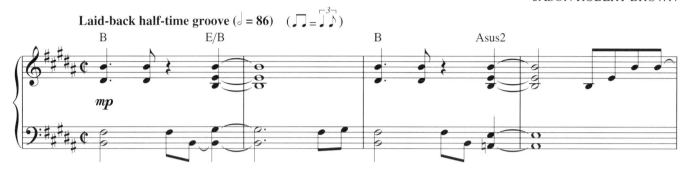

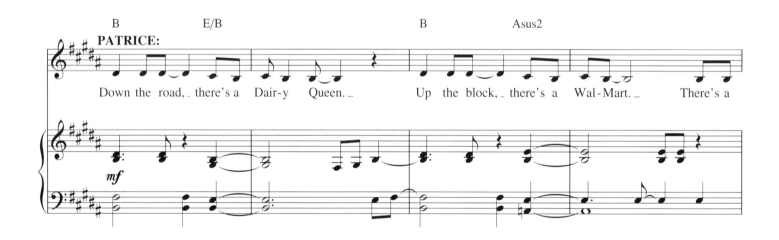

PATRICE:

Down the road, there's a Dair-y Queen. Up the block, there's a Wal-Mart. There's a

place you can ac-ces-so-rize your pets. A school,

alternative lyric: stu-pid

lam - est place ___ in ___ the world. ___ But I'm pret - ty sure ___ It's

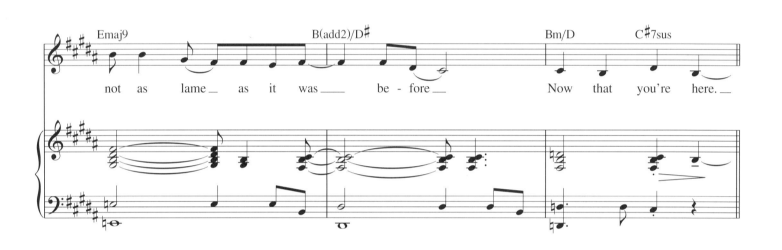

not as lame ___ as it was ___ be - fore ___ Now that you're here. ___

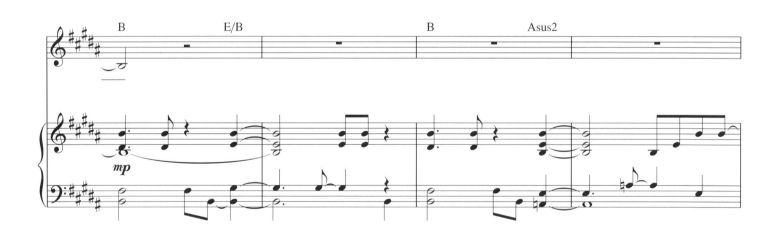

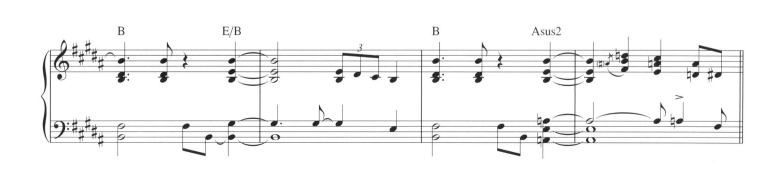

WHAT IT MEANS TO BE A FRIEND

from the Broadway Musical *13*

Music and Lyrics by
JASON ROBERT BROWN

POPULAR
from the Broadway Musical *Wicked*

Music and Lyrics by
STEPHEN SCHWARTZ

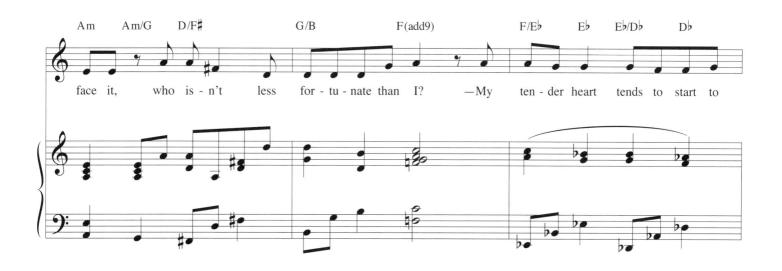

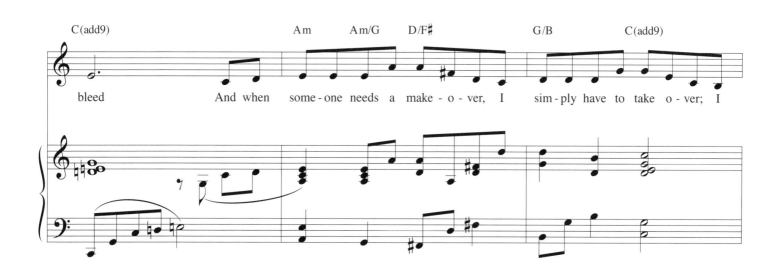

197

I'M NOT THAT GIRL

from the Broadway Musical *Wicked*

Music and Lyrics by
STEPHEN SCHWARTZ

Sweet and steady, like a music box

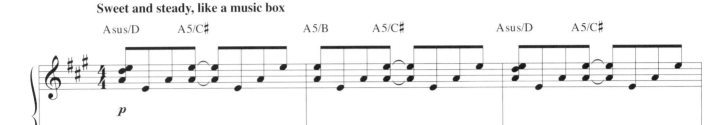

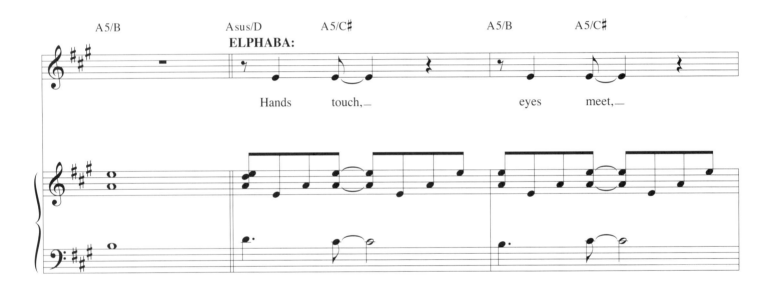

Hands touch, — eyes meet, —

Sud-den si - lence, sud-den heat. — Hearts leap — in a gid-dy

DEFYING GRAVITY
from the Broadway Musical *Wicked*

Music and Lyrics by
STEPHEN SCHWARTZ

206

COME TO YOUR SENSES

from *tick, tick... BOOM!*

Words and Music by
JONATHAN LARSON

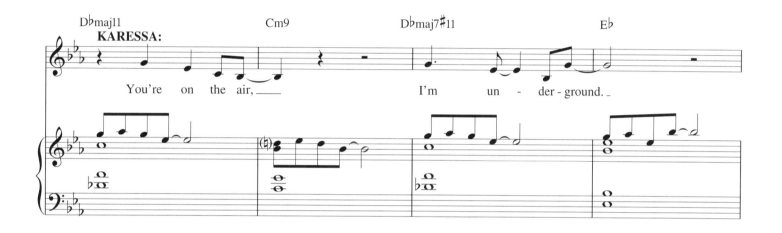

You're on the air, ___ I'm un - der - ground.

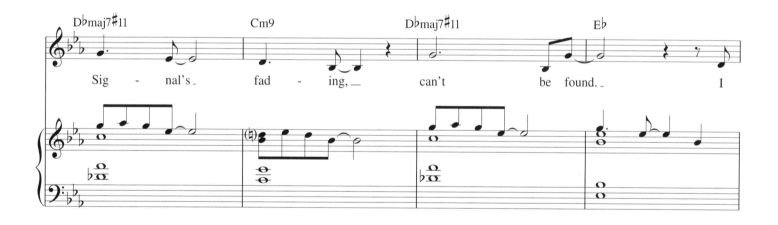

Sig - nal's ___ fad - ing, ___ can't be found. ___ I

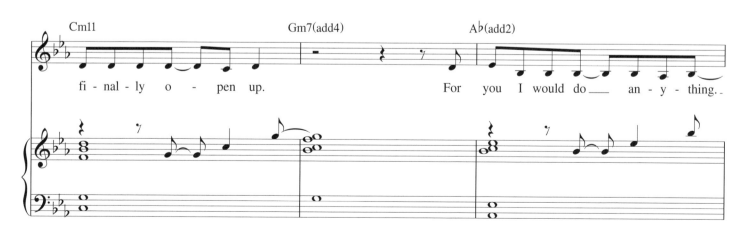

fi - nal - ly o - pen up. For you I would do ___ an - y - thing.

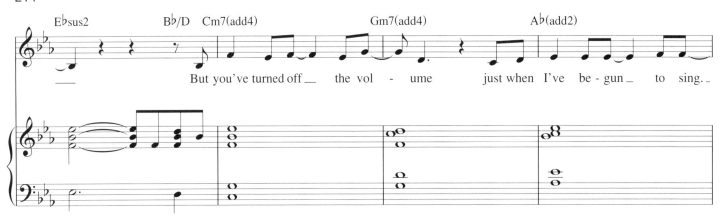

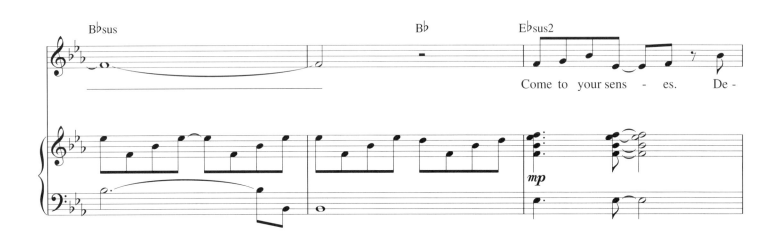

cold.   Noth-ing lasts __ an - y - more. __

Love be - comes __ dis-pos - a - ble. This is the shape __ of things we can not __

ig - nore. __

Majestically

Come to your sens - es. Sus - pense __

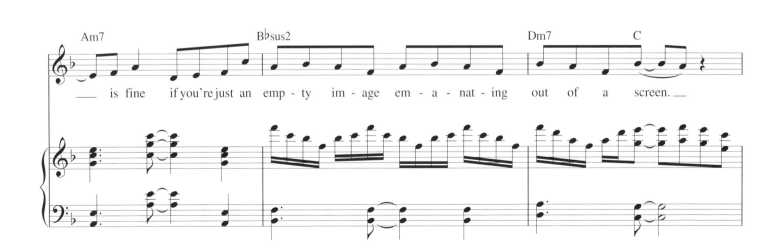

__ is fine if you're just an emp - ty im - age em - a - nat - ing out of a screen. __

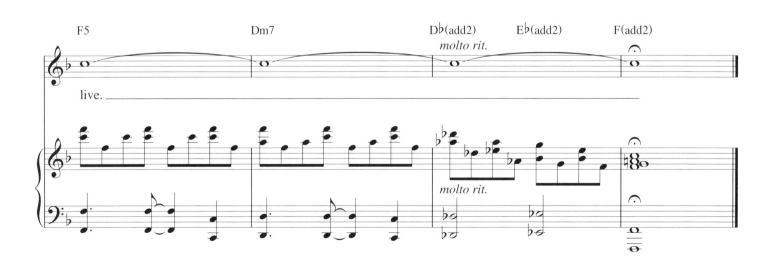

MY NEW PHILOSOPHY

from *You're a Good Man, Charlie Brown*

Words and Music by
ANDREW LIPPA

The song is a duet for Sally and Schroeder. The composer created this solo edition for publication.